EXERCISES IN ENGLISH

☆ GRAMMAR FOR LIFE ☆

LEVEL D

LOYOLAPRESS.
CHICAGO

Consultants
Therese Elizabeth Bauer
Martina Anne Erdlen
Anita Patrick Gallagher
Patricia Healey
Irene Kervick
Susan Platt

Linguistics Advisor
Timothy G. Collins
National-Louis University

Series Design: Karen Christoffersen
Cover Design: Vita Jay Schweighart
Cover Art: Jody Lepinot/prairiestudio.com
Cover Photoshop: Jerry Schweighart
Interior Art: Heather Kezdy
Character Education Portraits: Jim Mitchell
Back Cover Text: Ted Naron

Acknowledgments
page 139 — From *Webster's New World™ Children's Dictionary,* 2nd Edition. Copyright © 2000 by Hungry Minds, Inc. All rights reserved. Reproduced here by permission of the publisher.

page 141 — *The New Roget's Thesaurus in Dictionary Form,* Rev. Ed. New York: G. P. Putnam & Sons, 1978, p. 182.

0-8294-1743-5 ★

Manufactured in the United States of America.

08 Banta ★ 10 9 8 7

Table of Contents

Word Study Skills

Revising a Paragraph

Letter Writing

Research Skills

Name ______________________________

1. Identifying Sentences

A **sentence** is a group of words that expresses a complete thought. A sentence has a subject and a predicate. The subject is who or what the sentence is about. The predicate tells about the subject.

SUBJECT	PREDICATE
Most rain forests	**grow in the tropics.**

A. Read each example. Write **S** if the group of words is a sentence. Put a period at the end of each sentence.

_____ 1. Rain forests are hot and humid

_____ 2. Many kinds of plants and animals live in rain forests

_____ 3. Hundreds of different kinds of birds

_____ 4. The birds eat seeds, fruit, and insects

_____ 5. Nests in the tall trees

B. Make statements by matching the words in the first column with the words in the second column. Write the correct letter on the line. Use each letter once.

1. The sun shines _____	a. contains solar energy.
2. Plants use _____	b. to get energy.
3. The food in plants _____	c. every day in the rain forest.
4. There is solar energy _____	d. sunshine to make food.
5. Animals eat plants _____	e. in a plant's leaves, stems, and roots.
6. An insect _____	f. by eating insects.
7. A bird can get energy _____	g. eats a leaf and gets energy.
8. Some snakes eat _____	h. are all part of the food chain.
9. All animals get _____	i. energy from food.
10. Plants and animals _____	j. birds and get energy.

Review

Name____

2. Identifying Declarative and Interrogative Sentences

A **declarative sentence** makes a statement. It ends with a period.

Gold is a very valuable metal.

An **interrogative sentence** asks a question. It ends with a question mark.

Do you know how gold is mined?

Every sentence begins with a capital letter.

A. Decide whether each sentence is declarative or interrogative. Write your answer on the line.

____________ 1. What happened on January 24, 1848?

____________ 2. Gold was found at the edge of a river in California.

____________ 3. By May the streets of San Francisco were almost empty.

____________ 4. Where had everyone gone?

____________ 5. Almost everyone had headed for the gold fields.

____________ 6. In 1849, 90,000 Americans journeyed to California.

____________ 7. Were they called Forty Niners?

____________ 8. The discovery of gold changed the course of history.

____________ 9. People came from all over the world to find riches.

____________ 10. How many do you think were disappointed?

B. Decide whether each sentence is declarative or interrogative. Write your answer on the line. Add the correct end punctuation.

____________ 1. Where is gold usually found

____________ 2. Gold can be found in veins in rocks

____________ 3. Sometimes gold is found in rivers or creeks

____________ 4. Why is gold so expensive

____________ 5. Gold is a very rare metal

Name ____

3. Forming Declarative and Interrogative Sentences

Review

A sentence has a subject and a predicate.

SUBJECT	PREDICATE
Potatoes	**are an important crop in Idaho.**
The environment there	**provides good growing conditions.**

An information question can begin with *who, what, when* or *where.*

Underline the predicate in each sentence. Then rewrite each information sentence as a question. Use the question word given.

1. Tubers are part of the underground stem system of a potato plant.
   What ____?
2. Potato plants store food in the tubers.
   Where ____?
3. The tuber is the edible part of the potato plant.
   What ____?
4. Ancient people of Peru developed a technique to freeze-dry potatoes.
   Who ____?
5. Europeans first saw potatoes in South America in the 1500s.
   When ____?
6. Spanish conquistadors took potatoes from South America to Europe.
   Who ____?
7. Later European settlers brought potatoes to North America.
   Who ____?
8. Thomas Jefferson served French fries in the White House.
   What ____?
9. Today the potato is the world's fourth-most-important food crop.
   What ____?
10. Potatoes are grown in 130 countries around the world.
    Where ____?

Review

Name____

4. Identifying Imperative and Exclamatory Sentences

An **imperative sentence** gives a command or makes a request. It ends with a period.

Try to eat a healthful diet.

An **exclamatory sentence** expresses strong emotion. It ends with an exclamation point.

Stir-fried food is delicious!

A. Decide whether each sentence is imperative or exclamatory. Write your answer on the line. Add the correct end punctuation.

1. ____________ Chop meat and vegetables into bite-sized pieces
2. ____________ Heat a small amount of oil in a skillet
3. ____________ Stir in the meat and vegetables
4. ____________ Be careful
5. ____________ Don't burn yourself

B. Rewrite each sentence as a command.

1. You can bake a potato with the rays of the sun on a very hot day.

____

2. You have to get a potato and a small basket lined with aluminum foil.

____

3. You should push a nail through the bottom of the basket.

____

4. You have to stick the potato on the nail.

____

5. You should turn the cooker to face the sun as it moves across the sky.

____

Name____

5. Identifying the Four Kinds of Sentences

A sentence can be declarative, interrogative, imperative, or exclamatory.

Put the correct punctuation mark at the end of each sentence.

1. Ida B. Wells was a schoolteacher in Tennessee
2. On May 4, 1884, she got on a train to go to work
3. The conductor told her to move out of the first-class coach
4. He said black people had to ride in the smoking car
5. Ida was furious
6. What could she do to help other black people
7. She decided to become a newspaper reporter
8. In 1892 some friends of hers were lynched by a mob
9. She was horrified
10. Ida wrote articles against lynching
11. She made speeches all over the United States and in England
12. Did her work have any effect
13. The federal government took action to protect black people
14. Ida also worked for the suffrage movement
15. She wanted all citizens to be able to vote

Ida B. Wells worked tirelessly for equal justice for all. *Give an example of how you can help to see that everyone is treated fairly.*

Name____

6. Identifying Subjects and Predicates

A sentence has a subject and a predicate. The subject is who or what the sentence is about. The predicate tells about the subject.

SUBJECT	PREDICATE
The Pony Express	**started on April 3, 1860.**
Relays of riders	**carried mail from Missouri to California.**

A. Underline the subject of each sentence.

1. More than 180 men rode for the Pony Express.
2. The Pony Express route was almost 2,000 miles long.
3. Each Pony Express rider covered 75 to 100 miles.

4. A fresh horse was provided every 10 to 15 miles.
5. The original cost of mailing a letter was $5.00 per ounce.

B. Choose the best word to complete the predicate of each sentence. Use each word once.

appeared	**became**	**carried**	**caught**	**commemorated**
galloped	**jumped**	**killed**	**lived**	**rode**

1. A riderless horse ________________ into the Pony Express station in Sacramento.
2. Eleven-year-old Broncho Charlie Miller ________________ the horse.
3. Its rider had been ________________ by Indians.
4. Broncho Charlie ________________ on the horse.
5. He ________________ the mail to Placerville.
6. Broncho Charlie ________________ the youngest Pony Express rider.
7. As a young man, Charlie ________________ in Buffalo Bill's Wild West Show.
8. At age 81, he ________________ on horseback from New York to San Francisco.
9. The ride ________________ the 70th anniversary of the Pony Express.
10. Broncho Charlie ________________ to be 105 years old.

Name________________________________

7. Reviewing Sentences

Review

A. Read each example. Write S if the words form a sentence. Put a period at the end of each sentence.

_____ 1. Rainbows are created by light and water

_____ 2. The observer's back must be to the sun

_____ 3. Shines into the raindrops

_____ 4. The raindrops act as prisms

_____ 5. The light is refracted into many colors

B. Read each sentence. Draw a vertical line between the subject and the predicate.

1. The red-eyed tree frog is a very colorful animal.
2. Its most startling characteristic is its huge red eyes.
3. The body of the frog is mostly green, with splashes of blue or yellow.
4. The upper legs are usually bright blue.
5. The red-eyed tree frog's feet are orange or red.
6. These colors can darken with the frog's mood.
7. The tree frog depends on its feet for survival.
8. Its feet have suction-cup toe pads.
9. The toe pads cling to leaves, branches, and tree trunks.
10. This unusual creature lives in the rain forests of Central and South America.

CONTINUED

Review

Name____________________

C. Decide whether each sentence is declarative, interrogative, imperative, or exclamatory. Write your answer on the line. Put the correct punctuation mark at the end of each sentence.

__________ 1. Have you observed lightning during a storm

__________ 2. You always see lightning before you hear thunder

__________ 3. A lightning flash releases heat into the air

__________ 4. The warm air expands with a small explosion

__________ 5. Why do you see the lightning first

__________ 6. Light waves travel faster than sound waves

__________ 7. Count the seconds between the lightning and thunder

__________ 8. Divide the number of seconds by five

__________ 9. The answer is the distance of the storm in miles

__________ 10. Wow, that's interesting

Try It Yourself

Write four sentences about a storm you have witnessed. Be sure each sentence is complete. Use correct punctuation.

____

____

____

____

Check Your Own Work

Choose a piece of writing from your portfolio, a work in progress, an assignment from another class, or a letter. Revise it, applying the skills you have reviewed. The checklist will help you.

✔ Does each sentence express a complete thought?

✔ Does each sentence start with a capital letter?

✔ Does each sentence end with the correct punctuation?

Name ______________________________

8. Working with Subjects

Every sentence has two important parts. These parts are called the subject and the predicate. The **subject** names the person, place, or thing talked about in the sentence. The most important word in the subject is usually a noun. This noun is the **simple subject**. To find the subject, ask the question *who* or *what* before the predicate.

SUBJECT

The cool, fresh air is made up of matter.
(*What* is made up of matter?)

SIMPLE SUBJECT

This matter is a mixture of gases.
(*What* is a mixture of gases?)

Underline the simple subject in each sentence.

1. Air is tasteless and odorless.
2. Our precious air is also invisible.
3. Gases make up air.
4. All gases take up space and have weight.
5. Gases are made up of tiny particles.
6. These tiny particles are called molecules.
7. The molecules are moving constantly.
8. Nitrogen makes up most of the air, about 78 percent.
9. Oxygen makes up about 21 percent of the air.
10. Other gases make up 1 percent of the air.
11. Earthly life is possible because of these gases.
12. Plants use carbon dioxide to make food.
13. This process is called photosynthesis.
14. Oxygen is produced during photosynthesis.
15. All people need oxygen to breathe.

Name____

9. Working with Predicates

Sentences

Every sentence has two important parts. These parts are called the subject and the predicate. The **predicate** tells something about the subject and contains a verb. The verb is the important word in the predicate. The verb is called the **simple predicate**. To find the predicate, ask the question *do what* or *does what* after the subject.

PREDICATE

Explorers travel to other lands. (Explorers *do what*?)

SIMPLE PREDICATE

They often write about their adventures. (They *do what*?)

A. Underline the predicate twice in each sentence.

1. Marco Polo grew up in Venice, Italy, in the 13th century.
2. He wanted a life of adventure.
3. In 1271 he set out on an overland journey to China.
4. After many new and strange experiences, he reached China in 1275.
5. The ruler, Kublai Khan, appointed Marco Polo as an envoy.

B. Underline the simple predicate twice in each sentence.

1. Later on, Marco Polo served as governor of Yangchow for three years.
2. He even fought in battles, such as the one at Sainfu.
3. He returned to Venice with a treasure box of jewels in 1295.
4. The Genoese captured him in a battle.
5. While a captive, he wrote an account of his travels and adventures.

C. Match the subjects in the first column with the predicates in the second column. Write the correct letter on the line.

_____	1. Explorers	a. interest many people even today.
_____	2. Marco Polo	b. met Kublai Khan there.
_____	3. He	c. captured Marco Polo.
_____	4. The Genoese	d. visit other lands.
_____	5. His adventures	e. traveled to China.

Name________________________________

10. Working with Direct Objects

The **direct object** is the noun or pronoun that completes the action of the verb. Many sentences need a direct object to complete their meaning. To find the direct object of a sentence, ask *whom* or *what* after the verb. Sometimes there is more than one direct object. This is called a **compound direct object**.

DIRECT OBJECT

The first cars scared many people. (Cars scared *whom*?)

COMPOUND DIRECT OBJECT

People once drove horses and buggies. (People drove *what*?)

A. Circle the direct object in each sentence.

1. The first cars worried townspeople.
2. Some towns soon passed speed-limit laws.
3. Cars could not exceed four miles per hour.
4. Towns didn't have street signs.
5. They installed the street signs right away.
6. Henry Ford loved the idea of cars.
7. Happily, he watched other people in cars.
8. One day people would buy cars.
9. He opened a factory to build cars.
10. He started the Ford Motor Company in 1903.

B. Complete each sentence with a direct object from the list. Use each word once.

car **method** **Model T's** **step** **time**

1. In Ford's factory, workers built ________.
2. One worker did not build an entire ________.
3. Instead, each person on the assembly line did just one ________ in the process.
4. One worker's repetition of the same job saved ________ and money.
5. Now most factories use the assembly-line ________.

Name____

11. Subjects, Simple Predicates, and Direct Objects

A. Write **S** above the simple subject, **SP** above the simple predicate, and **DO** above the direct object in each sentence.

1. Many people use animals as a way of life.
2. The Sami people of the Arctic Circle herd reindeer.
3. These people follow their reindeer herds up and down mountains and valleys.
4. In summer the reindeer eat grasses in the mountains.
5. In winter the Sami bring their herds down to lower ground for food.
6. The Sami put marks of ownership on their reindeer's ears.
7. Each Sami family takes full advantage of its reindeer.
8. Sami wives make clothing with the softened skin.
9. Sami wives make tools with the bones of the reindeer.
10. These women also prepare reindeer meat as food.

B. Complete each sentence with a simple subject, a simple predicate, or a direct object.

1. A ________________ in the field scared the birds away.
2. The farmer's wife planted ________________ in the garden.
3. The farmer ________________ the corn in the fall.
4. The ________________ in the barn give lots of milk every morning.
5. Horses eat ________________ in their stalls.

Name ____

12. Compound Subjects

A **compound subject** has two or more simple subjects.

SIMPLE SUBJECT

A <u>moose</u> eats twigs and leaves.

COMPOUND SIMPLE SUBJECT

<u>Moose</u> and <u>deer</u> eat twigs and leaves.

A. Underline each noun in the subject.

1. Biologists and zoologists observe animal life.
2. Walruses, whales, and sea lions are large mammals.
3. Seals, reindeer, and elephants live in family groups called herds.
4. Sharks and piranhas attack with their sharp teeth.
5. Female wallabies and koalas keep their young in pouches.
6. Gophers and badgers live in burrows under the ground.
7. Snails and clams are both classified as mollusks.
8. Frogs, toads, and salamanders live in wet environments.
9. Oysters and mussels have protective hard shells.
10. Penguins and polar bears have adapted to very cold climates.

B. Combine each group of sentences into one sentence with a compound simple subject. Add correct end punctuation.

1 Dodo birds are now extinct. Auks are now extinct.

____

2. Dogs can dream. Cats can dream.

____

3. Spiders are not insects. Centipedes are not insects.

____

4. Hamsters are kept as pets. Gerbils are kept as pets.

____

5. Horses have hooves. Donkeys have hooves. Mules have hooves.

____

Name ____

13. Compound Predicates

A **compound predicate** has more than one simple predicate.

SIMPLE PREDICATE

A teacher instructs students.

COMPOUND SIMPLE PREDICATE

A seamstress cuts and sews cloth.

A. Underline the compound simple predicate twice in each sentence.

1. A gardener weeds and waters plants.
2. A nurse cleans and bandages wounds.
3. A scientist conducts and reports experiments.
4. A rodeo cowboy rides and ropes animals.
5. An administrative assistant answers the phone, sends faxes, and types letters.

B. Write complete sentences with compound simple predicates.

1. An artist ____

____

2. A farmer ____

____

3. A basketball player ____

____

4. A student ____

____

5. I ____

____

Name____

14. Reviewing Sentences

A. Underline the simple subject in each sentence.

1. Elizabeth Blackwell was born in 1821 in Bristol, England.
2. Elizabeth had four sisters and four brothers.
3. At that time most girls did not receive good educations.
4. Elizabeth's father hired fine private tutors for her and her sisters.
5. Elizabeth's education would help her in the future.

B. Underline the simple predicate twice in each sentence.

1. In Elizabeth's eleventh year the family moved to the United States.
2. After her father's death the family needed money.
3. Elizabeth and her sisters gave music and English lessons to local children.
4. Elizabeth helped many people.
5. One day Elizabeth visited a sick woman.

C. Circle the direct object in each sentence.

1. Elizabeth's sick friend had a secret.
2. Her male doctors didn't understand women well.
3. She presented an idea to Elizabeth.
4. Elizabeth would pursue a career in medicine.
5. Sixteen medical schools denied Elizabeth admission.

CONTINUED

Name____

D. Underline the compound simple predicate twice in each sentence.

1. Finally she successfully argued and won her case for admission.
2. A college in New York explained the situation and asked its students to vote on admission for Elizabeth.
3. Probably as a joke, the all-male student body voted and accepted her.
4. Elizabeth studied hard and graduated from medical school.
5. She imagined and then founded the first women's medical college.

Elizabeth Blackwell fought for fair treatment of women.
Give an example of something you can do to help society be fair to women.

Try It Yourself

Write four sentences about helping with a chore around the house. Include direct objects, at least one compound simple subject, and at least one compound simple predicate.

____

____

____

____

Check Your Own Work

Choose a piece of writing from your portfolio, a work in progress, an assignment from another class, or a letter. Revise it, using the skills you have reviewed. The checklist will help you.

✔ Do your sentences express a complete thought?

✔ Have you used direct objects objects correctly?

✔ Were you able to use compound subjects or predicates in your sentences?

Name ____

15. Identifying Nouns

A **noun** names a person, place, or thing.

Animals use different parts of their bodies for different needs.

A. Underline the nouns in each sentence.

1. African elephants use their big ears to help them cool down.
2. Blood passes through their ears and sends heat out into the air.
3. Hungry elephants can use their tusks to break apart trees to get to the soft pulp inside.
4. Thirsty elephants use them to dig for water in dry ground.
5. After they find water, elephants scoop it up with their trunks and put it in their mouths.
6. Polar bears live in regions covered in snow and ice.
7. These bears use their thick fur to stay warm.
8. The fur of a polar bear is really clear, not white.
9. Sunlight passes through the clear fur down to the bear's skin.
10. The bear's skin is dark and takes in the heat from the sun.

B. Complete each sentence with a noun or nouns. Use each word once.

bat	**homes**	**blood**	**poison**	**eggs**
ground	**spaces**	**holes**	**teeth**	

1. Many animals use their ________ in interesting ways.
2. A vampire ________ uses its sharp teeth to drink ________.
3. Some snakes shoot ________ through hollow ________ in their teeth (fangs) to kill other animals.
4. Other snakes make ________ in ________ to suck out the soft yolk inside.
5. Gophers use their big front teeth to help dig their ________ in the ________.

Name____

16. Identifying Proper and Common Nouns

A **proper noun** names a particular person, place, or thing. A **common noun** names any one member of a group of persons, places, or things.

PROPER NOUNS

Our planet Earth has many different climates and habitats.
A single country, such as Spain, can also have different climates and habitats.

COMMON NOUNS

Earth has many different climates and habitats.
A single country, such as Spain, can also have different climates and habitats.

A. Underline each proper noun. Circle each common noun.

1. The United States has many different regions with different kinds of weather.
2. What is the climate like where you live?
3. Polar bears live in the cold climate of Alaska.
4. The flat plains of Kansas are used to grow wheat.
5. In a desert it is very hot and dry during the day.
6. The Mojave Desert is in parts of California and Arizona.
7. Large amounts of rain fall in the state of Washington.
8. The state of Minnesota has many lakes.
9. Florida is home to the Everglades, a warm and wet swamp.
10. The Rocky Mountains are famous for their beauty in winter.

B. Match a proper noun from the first column with the related common noun from the second column. Write the correct letter on the line.

_____	1. Pacific	a. building
_____	2. George Washington	b. amusement park
_____	3. Utah	c. president
_____	4. White House	d. state
_____	5. Disney World	e. ocean

Name______________________________

17. Identifying Singular and Plural Nouns

A **singular noun** names one person, place, or thing.
A **plural noun** names more than one person, place, or thing.
The plural of most nouns is formed by adding *-s* or *-es* to the singular. The plural of a noun ending in *y* after a vowel is formed by adding *-s*. To form the plural of a noun ending in *y* after a consonant, change the *y* to *i* and add *-es*.
The plural of some nouns is irregular.

SINGULAR NOUNS

An apple a day keeps the doctor away.

PLURAL NOUNS

Of all the fruits, strawberries were what the boys wanted.

A. Write **S** on the line if each noun is singular or **P** if each noun is plural.

1. peaches ______
2. grape ______
3. berries ______
4. plums ______
5. banana ______
6. onion ______
7. peppers ______
8. tomatoes ______
9. carrot ______
10. beans ______

B. Write the plural for each singular noun.

1. seal ________________
2. daisy ________________
3. cherry ________________
4. violet ________________
5. kite ________________
6. fairy ________________
7. paint ________________
8. story ________________
9. jury ________________
10. dish ________________

Name____

18. Working with Singular and Plural Nouns

Nouns

A. Circle each singular noun. Underline each plural noun.

1. Never play with matches.
2. Do not lean out of an open window.
3. Lock up all medicines in a safe place.
4. Turn out all lights before leaving the house.
5. Do not put metal in the microwave.
6. Don't leave a room where water is running.
7. Lock the cabinet or closet where detergents are kept.
8. Do not open the front door to strangers.
9. Keep perishable foods in the refrigerator.
10. Know where a flashlight is.

B. Complete each sentence with the plural of the noun at the left.

stair	1. Walk, don't run, on the ____________________.
compass	2. Be careful with sharp objects such as ____________________ and scissors.
door	3. Close classroom ____________________ quietly and slowly.
instruction	4. When there is a fire drill, follow your teacher's ____________________.
classmate	5. Be polite and respectful to your ____________________.
tool	6. Keep ____________________ in good order and in their proper places.
sport	7. When you play ____________________, follow the rules.
stranger	8. Report any ____________________ in the hallways to a teacher.
problem	9. Solve ____________________ with a classmate rather than argue.
class	10. Get to your ____________________ on time.

Name____

19. Using Singular Possessive Nouns

The possessive form of a noun shows **possession** or ownership. To form the **singular possessive**, add an apostrophe (') and the letter *s* (*'s*) to a singular noun.

A person's actions can have many consequences.

Rosa Parks's action changed American society.

Nouns

A. Underline the possessive noun in each sentence.

1. Rosa Parks's story began on December 1, 1955, on a public bus in Montgomery, Alabama.
2. A white man's demand for her seat on the bus upset her.
3. Rosa Parks's response to the man was a polite no.
4. The white man's reaction was to call the police.
5. Even being arrested couldn't change this determined woman's mind.

B. Write on the line the possessive form of each *italicized* singular noun.

__________ 1. News of Rosa *Parks* refusal to give up her seat spread .

__________ 2. *Rosa* arrest and trial became a symbol of injustice.

__________ 3. The African American *community* response was swift.

__________ 4. A boycott of *Montgomery* bus system was organized.

__________ 5. The black *community* boycott lasted 381 days.

__________ 6. *Alabama* governor was forced to pay attention.

__________ 7. *Parks* case went all the way to the Supreme Court.

__________ 8. The Supreme *Court* ruling said that segregation was unconstitutional.

__________ 9. Parks is forever a part of *America* history.

__________ 10. A *person* action in the cause of justice can indeed change people's lives.

Rosa Parks fought for equal treatment under the law for all people. Give an example of how you can work for fair and equal treatment for everyone.

Name____

20. Working with Singular Possessive Nouns

Underline the noun in each sentence that should be in singular possessive form. Write the possessive form on the line.

America's — Most of America states have adopted an official bird, tree, and flower.

______________ 1. Mom favorite bird is the cardinal, the Kentucky state bird.

______________ 2. The robin is Michigan state bird.

______________ 3. New York bluebird appears on the stamp.

______________ 4. Florida official bird is the mockingbird.

______________ 5. The southern pine is Arkansas official tree.

______________ 6. South Carolina official tree is the palmetto.

______________ 7. The hemlock adoptive state is Pennsylvania.

______________ 8. Illinois violet appears on the travel brochure.

______________ 9. I have never seen Alabama official flower, the camellia.

______________ 10. Among Hawaii flowers is the hibiscus, the state flower.

______________ 11. California redwoods grow taller than you can imagine.

______________ 12. The dogwood blossoms can be seen throughout Missouri in the spring.

______________ 13. The postcard from Tennessee showed the iris bright yellow and blue.

______________ 14. Dad love of the chickadee started when he moved to Massachusetts.

______________ 15. Which state flower is your favorite?

Name____

21. Using Plural Possessive Nouns

To form the **plural possessive**, add an apostrophe (') after the *-s* of the plural form. When a plural does not end in *-s*, add an apostrophe and *s* (*'s*).

SINGULAR NOUN	**A circus performer must be physically fit.**
PLURAL NOUN	**Circus performers travel around the country.**
PLURAL POSSESSIVE NOUN	**Circus performers' lives must be interesting!**
SINGULAR NOUN	**The child held the red balloon.**
PLURAL NOUN	**The children held the balloons.**
PLURAL POSSESSIVE NOUN	**The children's balloons were many colors.**

A. Complete the chart with the plural form and the plural possessive form of each word.

	PLURAL	PLURAL POSSESSIVE
1. ringmaster	____________	the ____________ tall hats
2. lion tamer	____________	the ____________ whips
3. clown	____________	the ____________ smiles
4. trapeze artist	____________	the ____________ nets
5. elephant	____________	the ____________ trunks

B. Write on the line the possessive form of the *italicized* plural noun.

____________ 1. My *grandparents* surprise was a trip to the circus!

____________ 2. I loved seeing all the circus *performers* acts.

____________ 3. My older *brothers* favorites were the trained animals.

____________ 4. I preferred watching the *clowns* crazy stunts.

____________ 5. My grandparents enjoyed the *magicians* tricks.

Nouns

Name______________________________

22. Working with Plural Possessive Nouns

Underline the noun in each sentence that should be in plural possessive form. On the line write the plural possessive form.

Nouns

workers'	**In a movie studio all the workers jobs are important.**
__________	1. The set carpenters jobs are to build realistic interior sets.
__________	2. Actors are turned into aliens and monsters through make-up artists skills.
__________	3. Subtitlers translations for foreign films can be seen at the bottom of movie screens.
__________	4. Location managers responsibilities include finding shooting sites.
__________	5. Hanging microphones out of camera range is the boom men job.
__________	6. The sound editors work includes putting together all the sounds except music for the movie sound track.
__________	7. Movie plots and characters seem real because of the actors portrayals.
__________	8. Camera operators main responsibilities include making sure the cameras are working properly.
__________	9. Among the color timers jobs is making sure colors look the same in each shot.
__________	10. Period costumes and everyday clothes alike are the costume designers responsibilities.

Name____

23. Identifying Nouns Used as Subjects

A noun may be used as the subject of a sentence. The subject tells what the sentence is about. The subject tells *who* or *what* does something or is something.

Pollution affects our environment.
(*What* affects our environment?)

People pollute our air, land, and water.
(*Who* pollutes our air, land, and water?)

Nouns

A. Find the subject by answering the question beside the sentence. Underline the subject.

1. Some factories release smoke. — *What* releases smoke?
2. Smoke makes the air dirty. — *What* makes the air dirty?
3. People throw trash in empty lots. — *Who* throws trash?
4. Some farmers use harmful chemicals. — *Who* uses chemicals?
5. Factories dump dirty water into rivers. — *What* dumps dirty water?

B. Underline the subject in each sentence. Write on the line whether it answers *who* or *what*.

1. The exhaust from cars pollutes the air. ____________
2. Chemicals in the rivers kill fish. ____________
3. Oil spills pollute the ocean and marine life. ____________
4. Caring citizens clean up the environment. ____________
5. Laws can help protect our environment. ____________

Name____

24. Using Nouns as Direct Objects

A noun may be used as the direct object of a sentence. The direct object tells *whom* or *what* receives the action of the verb.

People admire inventors.
(People admire *whom?*)

Alexander Graham Bell invented the first telephone.
(Alexander Graham Bell invented *what?*)

Nouns

A. Find the direct object by answering the question beside each sentence. Underline the direct object.

1. Edison and Swan sold the first light bulb. — Edison and Swan sold *what?*
2. Fox designed the umbrella in 1874. — Fox designed *what?*
3. Mrs. Cockran made the first dishwasher. — Mrs. Cockran made *what?*
4. Raytheon created the microwave oven. — Raytheon created *what?*
5. Inventions help people. — Inventions help *whom?*

B. Underline the direct object in each sentence. Write on the line whether it answers the question *whom* or *what*.

1. Sometimes people wanted entertainment. ______________
2. In 1844 Sax invented the saxophone. ______________
3. In 1847 Ingram sold blow-up party balloons. ______________
4. Blackton produced the first animated cartoon. ______________
5. These inventions delighted young people. ______________

Name____

25. Reviewing Nouns

A. **Underline each proper noun. Circle each common noun.**

1. There are many kinds of natural disasters.
2. One famous natural disaster happened long ago, in A.D. 79.
3. Mount Vesuvius, a volcano in Italy, erupted.
4. The lava and ash from the volcano buried the city of Pompeii.
5. Archaeologists discovered the ruins of Pompeii and another city called Herculaneum in the eighteenth century.

Nouns

B. **Write S in the parentheses if the *italicized* noun is singular or P if it is plural.**

1. Forest *fires* (   ) are another *kind* (   ) of natural *disaster* (   ).
2. *Trees* (   ) and *plants* (   ) in the *forest* (   ) dry out when there isn't enough rain.
3. A single *bolt* (   ) of lightning can cause fires that destroy whole *forests* (   ).
4. The *flames* (   ) can also destroy animals and even houses in the *area* (   ).
5. In *emergencies* (   ) like these, firefighters spend *days* (   ) trying to put out the fire.

C. **Complete each sentence with the singular or plural possessive form of the noun at the left.**

hurricane 1. A ______________________ direction and speed can change quickly.

driver 2. A ______________________ best protection in a tornado is to get under a bridge.

children 3. The ______________________ boat was carried downstream by the flood.

experts 4. The ______________________ opinions on the force of the earthquake varied.

Earthquakes 5. ______________________ damage can be severe.

Name______________________________

D. Underline the simple subject and circle the direct object(s) in each sentence.

1. Many people build homes in villages near volcanoes.
2. Volcanoes may destroy their homes.
3. But these people will risk the destruction of their homes for economic reasons.
4. The land's rich soil promises good crops for farmers.
5. A volcano's eruptions create new land and rich soil.

Nouns

Try It Yourself

Imagine a flood in your town. Write four sentences about the flood. Include a simple subject in each sentence. Include at least one example of a direct object and one example of a possessive noun in your sentences.

____

____

____

____

Check Your Own Work

Choose a piece of writing from your portfolio, a work in progress, an assignment from another class, or a letter. Revise it, using the skills you have reviewed. The checklist will help you.

✔ Have you capitalized all proper nouns?

✔ Have you followed the rules you learned for plural nouns?

✔ Have you used the apostrophe correctly for possessive nouns?

Name ______________________________

26. Identifying Personal Pronouns

A **personal pronoun** is a word that takes the place of a noun. Personal pronouns are *I, me, we, us, you, he, him, she, her, it, they,* and *them.*

NOUN **Who were the pioneers?**

PRONOUN **They were people who traveled to the American West.**

A. Underline the personal pronoun(s) in each sentence.

1. Where did they come from?
2. They came from the eastern states and from far away.
3. It was a long time ago, in the nineteenth century.
4. Mom told me that Great-great-grandfather came from Sweden.
5. He brought two cousins with him.
6. He didn't bring a wife?
7. Well, not right away. She didn't want to come at first.
8. Did he finally convince her to come?
9. Yes. She brought Great-great-grandfather's dog with her too.
10. Well, I'm sure he was happy to see them both!

B. In each pair of sentences, some pronouns are *italicized.* Circle the nouns they refer to in the sentences.

1. Pioneers had to plan their trip west very carefully.
   They had to take all necessary supplies with *them.*
2. Each pioneer family had a wagon.
   Everything had to fit into *it.*
3. The pioneers had to bring seeds.
   They needed *them* to grow food.
4. People had to bring tools to make furniture.
   They couldn't make *it* without tools.
5. Weapons were important too.
   If a man lost *them,* he couldn't hunt or defend himself.

Name______________________________

27. Understanding Personal Pronouns: The Speaker

A personal pronoun names the speaker, the person spoken to, or the person or thing spoken about. The personal pronouns that name the speaker are *I, me, we,* and *us.*

At our school, teachers and students enjoy field trips.
At our school, we enjoy field trips.

Pronouns

A. Circle the pronoun that names the speaker in each sentence.

1. We went to see the new planetarium at the museum.
2. Our teacher showed us where to leave our coats and backpacks.
3. A special guide explained the tour to us.
4. I didn't know the solar system was so big.
5. We counted many moons around some of the planets.
6. The guide invited me to visit the planetarium again.
7. I would definitely come back someday.
8. We collected our things and went back to school.
9. What did I like best?
10. I liked Saturn because of its many rings.

B. Complete each sentence with a pronoun that names the speaker.

1. The teacher wants ________ to do reports on the planets.
2. ________ want to report on the planet Saturn, and so does Toshi.
3. ________ will work together on our report.
4. ________ want to talk about Titan, one of Saturn's 21 moons.
5. Titan is interesting to ________ because it is the biggest moon, bigger than the planets Mercury and Pluto!

Name ____________________

28. Understanding Personal Pronouns: The Person Spoken To

The personal pronoun that names the person or persons spoken to is *you*. *You* can be either singular or plural.

Would you like something to eat?

A. Circle the pronouns that name the person(s) spoken to in the sentences.

1. How do you know that you are hungry?
2. By growling, your stomach tells you that it's time to eat.
3. You also know that it's time to eat when your energy is gone.
4. You need to eat about every four hours during the day.
5. After you eat, the process of digestion begins.
6. You begin to digest food in your mouth, as your saliva makes it soft.
7. The food you have chewed and softened goes down the esophagus.
8. Your stomach then breaks down the food into a liquid, so that you receive its nutrients.
9. The nutrients in the food supply you with energy.
10. When you feel tired again, it's probably time to eat!

B. Write an **S** on the line if *you* is singular or **P** if it is plural. Use other words in the sentence to help you decide.

_____ 1. Class, you may go outside for recess now.

_____ 2. Do you have your umbrellas or raincoats?

_____ 3. Sally, you cannot go out without some rain protection.

_____ 4. Mrs. Struthers, do you have an extra umbrella?

_____ 5. You are in luck, Sally, I do.

Name________________________________

29. Understanding Personal Pronouns: The Person or Thing Spoken About

The personal pronouns that name the person(s) or thing(s) spoken about are *he, him, she, her, it, they,* and *them.*

When people see injustice, they work hard to stop it.

Circle the pronouns that name the person(s) or thing(s) spoken about in each example.

1. Harriet Tubman was born in Maryland in 1821. She was a slave who escaped to freedom.
2. Harriet Tubman knew that other people wanted to be free, so she decided to help them.
3. She made over fifteen different trips to the South.
4. Harriet Tubman made very careful plans, so that nothing would happen to her or to the people she was helping.
5. When people came to her, she gave them clothes, passes, and train tickets.
6. She told the slaves about different homes and churches where they could hide as they traveled to freedom.
7. These homes and churches became the secret Underground Railroad, and many slaves soon knew about it.
8. She helped between 200 and 300 people escape from slavery.
9. During the Civil War she worked for the Union Army, helping it by working as a scout, a cook, and a nurse.
10. Some people compared her to Moses in the Bible, who led people to freedom.

Harriet Tubman put herself in danger to help others lead better lives. Give an example of what you can do to help people lead better lives.

Name____

30. Using Singular and Plural Pronouns

A **singular personal pronoun** refers to one person, place, or thing. The singular personal pronouns are *I, me, you, he, him, she, her,* and *it.* A **plural personal pronoun** refers to more than one person, place, or thing. The plural personal pronouns are *we, us, you, they,* and *them.*

SINGULAR PERSONAL PRONOUN	**He is interested in animals.**
PLURAL PERSONAL PRONOUN	**Animals are important to us in many ways.**

Pronouns

Circle the pronoun in each sentence. Write **S** on the line if it is singular and **P** if it is plural.

_____ 1. Some animals help us in strange ways.

_____ 2. One animal, the leech, looks like a worm, but it is different.

_____ 3. It has a mouth that acts like a suction cup.

_____ 4. A leech also has teeth and uses them to attach to another animal.

_____ 5. You might know that long ago doctors attached leeches to sick people to cure them.

_____ 6. They thought the leeches would suck out the sickness.

_____ 7. Doctors don't believe that anymore, but they are still interested in leeches, because leech saliva stops blood from clotting.

_____ 8. Clotting helps us by stopping bleeding.

_____ 9. But clots can be dangerous to you because they can form inside the brain or heart.

_____10. Learning how leeches can stop clots may help us prevent strokes and heart attacks.

Name____

31. Using Pronouns as Subjects

A personal pronoun may be used as the subject of a sentence. The subject pronouns are *I, we, you, he, she, it,* and *they*.

SIMPLE SUBJECT	**Magnets help us in many ways.**
SUBJECT PRONOUN	**They improve our lives.**

Pronouns

A. Underline the subject pronoun in each sentence.

1. Do you know much about magnets?
2. I learned about magnets in school.
3. They attract metal objects, such as nails or paper clips.
4. We call this special attraction magnetism.
5. It is a valuable force people can use in many ways.
6. In our kitchens we use magnets to hold messages on the refrigerators.
7. They are used in hospitals in special MRI machines.
8. In maglev trains they keep the trains off the rails and in the air.
9. Did you know Earth is a magnet too?
10. It has north and south magnetic poles.

B. Look at the word(s) on the left and then write a sentence. Use a subject pronoun that takes the place of the word or words.

1. (magnets) ____
2. (Earth) ____
3. (your science teacher) ____
4. (you and your classmates) ____
5. (your science class) ____

Name____

32. Using Pronouns as Direct Objects

A personal pronoun may be used as the direct object in a sentence. The object pronouns are *me, us, you, him, her, it,* and *them.*

Direct Object Noun	**In the United States, citizens choose their leaders.**
Direct Object Pronoun	**They choose them through government elections.**

A. Underline the object pronoun in each sentence except the *italicized* sentence.

1. *The election candidates stand on the platform.* We recognize them from TV.
2. They persuade us with speeches.
3. Posters and campaign buttons introduce them.
4. The reporters may interview you for a citizen's reaction to the speeches.
5. The candidates' promises interest me.

B. Write on the lines object pronouns that take the place of the *italicized* words.

1. Many people don't trust this *politician.* ________
2. People want the truth, and some people think he doesn't tell the *truth.* ________
3. I didn't like his ideas, and so I didn't watch the *politician* on TV. ________
4. As soon as the politician made his promise, he forgot the *promise.* ________
5. When they heard his speech, they trusted the *man* again. ________

Name____

33. Using I and Me

Use the word *I* to talk about yourself. *I* is used as the subject of a sentence. Use the word *me* to talk about yourself. *Me* is used as the direct object of a sentence.

SUBJECT **I am interested in the lives of Native Americans.**

DIRECT OBJECT **They interest me.**

Pronouns

Complete each sentence with the pronoun *I* or *me*.

1. _____ love to camp and hike.
2. Last summer _____ camped in the woods of northern Wisconsin.
3. A good friend accompanied _____.
4. _____ had trouble staking my tent to the ground.
5. He helped _____ with the staking.
6. Later he challenged _____ to an eight-hour hike with him.
7. _____ had never hiked so long before.
8. After the hike he photographed _____ massaging my feet.
9. He also examined _____ for ticks.
10. _____ thanked him for that.
11. At night _____ sat by the campfire.
12. _____ listened to its crackling.
13. My friend joined _____ by the flames.
14. He informed _____ of another great trail to hike.
15. _____ listened with excitement.

Name____

34. Using *We* and *Us*

Use the word *we* to talk about yourself and at least one other person. *We* is used as the subject of a sentence.
Use the word *us* to talk about yourself and at least one other person. *Us* is used as the direct object of a sentence.

SUBJECT **We get sick.**
DIRECT OBJECT **Doctors help us get better.**

Pronouns

Complete each sentence with the pronoun *we* or *us*.

1. Why do _____ get sick?
2. Does something attack _____ inside our bodies?
3. Doctors and scientists examine _____ for germs, bacteria, and viruses.
4. _____ don't see germs, bacteria, or viruses, because they are extremely small.
5. To see them, _____ have to look through powerful microscopes.
6. _____ need to protect ourselves from these tiny beings.
7. Doctors can direct _____ to the rules of good health.
8. To stay healthy, _____ need to eat well, get regular exercise, and get enough sleep.
9. These good habits help _____ stay strong and fight germs.
10. Sometimes, though, _____ get sick anyway.
11. Something infects _____.
12. It sends _____ to bed.
13. _____ nurse ourselves back to health slowly.
14. The doctor warns _____ not to do too much activity too soon.
15. _____ are so glad when we are healthy again.

Name____

35. Recognizing Possessive Pronouns

A **possessive pronoun** shows possession or ownership.
The possessive pronouns are *mine, yours, his, hers, its, ours,* and *theirs.*

My favorite food is peanut butter. What's yours?
Mine is tomato soup.

Pronouns

A. Underline the possessive pronoun in each group of sentences.

1. Grandpa's favorite actor was Bing Crosby. Who was Grandma's?
   Oh, hers was Bob Hope.
2. We've seen many movies, and our favorite one is *Citizen Kane.*
   Really? Ours too.
3. Which movie theater is your favorite?
   That new one on Spring Street is mine.
4. Their favorite snack at the movies is popcorn.
   Well, it's not ours; we like nachos.
5. Mom's favorite time to see a movie is in the evening. When is Dad's?
   His is in the afternoon.

B. Complete each sentence with the correct possessive pronoun.
The words in parentheses tell you which pronoun to use.

1. Gia and Howie entered their science project in a contest.
   ________ won second place! *(spoken about, plural)*
2. My rug project doesn't look anything like the Navajos' do!
   Does ________? *(spoken to, singular)*
3. I always like Moira's paintings. She's really good.
   Yes. ________ are so colorful and full of energy. *(spoken about, singular)*
4. Look at the paper Ken and Judy made!
   Wow! It's a bigger piece than ________. *(speaker, plural)*
5. Well, I'm no expert, but here's my clay pot.
   ________ is not finished yet. *(speaker, singular)*

Name____

36. Reviewing Pronouns

A. Circle the personal pronoun(s) in each sentence.

1. Most of us enjoy listening to or playing music.
2. I enjoy classical music, but my brother doesn't.
3. He likes to listen to popular music on the radio.
4. My sister likes that kind of music too, so it doesn't bother her.
5. What kind of music do you enjoy?

B. Write on the line whether the *italicized* pronoun in each sentence names the speaker, the person or thing spoken to, or the person or thing spoken about.

1. *I* would like to learn more about folk music. ______________
2. Did *you* know every country has its own folk music? ______________
3. Some traditional songs are gone; no one remembers *them*.

   ____
4. Sometimes a musical instrument disappears, because no one is left to show how to play *it*. ______________
5. It is important for all of *us* to remember the music of the past.

   ____

C. Write **S** on the line if the *italicized* pronoun is singular or **P** if it is plural. Write **SP** above the *italicized* pronoun if it is a subject pronoun and **DO** if it is a direct object pronoun

_____ 1. You can take natural materials and use *them* to make music.

_____ 2. People can hollow out a log and beat *it* like a drum.

_____ 3. *They* can blow a shell to make a kind of trumpet sound.

_____ 4. *You* can fill gourds with seeds and stones to make a rattle.

_____ 5. *I* know how to make a flute from bamboo.

Name____

D. In the sentences below, circle the possessive pronouns.

1. I wish I had a voice like yours.
2. Mine squeaks and cracks when I sing.
3. Many singers take voice lessons to train theirs.
4. Hers is the softest voice I have ever heard.
5. His, so loud and booming, can be heard clearly from the back of the music hall.

Try It Yourself

Write four sentences about your own possessions and your family's possessions. Use possessive pronouns.

____

____

____

____

Check Your Own Work

Choose a piece of writing from your portfolio, a work in progress, an assignment from another class, or a letter. Revise it, using the skills you have reviewed. The checklist will help you.

✔ Have you chosen the correct subject pronouns and direct object pronouns to replace nouns?

✔ Were you careful when you used singular and plural pronouns?

✔ Have you used possessive pronouns correctly?

Name ______________________________

37. Identifying Adjectives

Adjectives are words that describe nouns. They tell what kind. Some adjectives come before nouns.

Scientists are careful observers of the world around them. They use descriptive language to record what they see.

A. Underline each adjective. Circle the noun that is described.

1. The egg was found in the side of a rocky cliff.
2. The scientist dug out the large, heavy egg.
3. It had a brown, leathery shell.
4. The egg had several tiny cracks.
5. A dinosaur laid the unusual egg.

B. Which adjectives from the list describe the words below on the left? Write them on the lines.

soft **breakable** **white** **splintery** **red**

glass 1. ______________

wood 2. ______________

fur 3. ______________

blood 4. ______________

teeth 5. ______________

C. Choose an animal. Use five adjectives to describe it.

Animal: ______________

1. ______________ 4. ______________

2. ______________ 5. ______________

3. ______________

Name____

38. Working with Adjectives

> Adjectives are words that describe nouns. They tell what kind.

A. Write a noun that could follow each pair of adjectives from a story.

1. old, evil ____________________
2. shy, beautiful ____________________
3. handsome, brave ____________________
4. dark, gloomy ____________________
5. long, dangerous ____________________

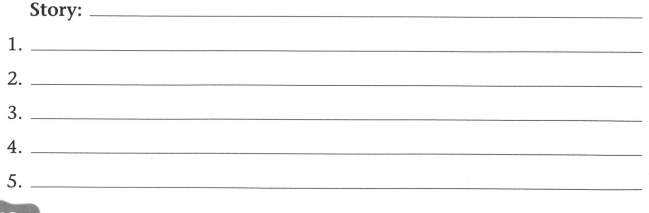

B. Underline the adjectives in each sentence. Write on the line whether they refer to the sense of *touch, taste, sight, smell,* or *hearing.*

__________ 1. The magician gave her a bitter liquid to drink.

__________ 2. The prince attacked with his shining sword.

__________ 3. The child stroked the dragon's cold and scaly head.

__________ 4. The damp, foul odor of the dungeon was everywhere.

__________ 5. The thundering hooves of many horses announced the soldiers' arrival.

C. Think about a favorite story of yours. Describe some of the people and actions in the story. Use adjectives that refer to the senses.

Story: ____

1. ____
2. ____
3. ____
4. ____
5. ____

Adjectives

Name____

39. Recognizing Proper Adjectives

Some adjectives are formed from proper nouns. These adjectives are called **proper adjectives**. All other adjectives are called **common adjectives**. A proper adjective begins with a capital letter.

PROPER NOUN	**France is famous for its many types of cheese.**
PROPER ADJECTIVE	**French cheese is exported to other countries.**

A. Underline the proper adjective in each sentence. Circle the noun it describes.

1. In the world marketplace Swiss watches are a popular product.
2. Valencia oranges from Spain are sold all over the world.
3. Italian olive oil is a popular import in the United States.
4. Japanese computer technology is another popular product.
5. American fast food is now available around the world.

B. Complete each sentence with a proper adjective formed from the proper noun on the left.

Korea	1. Have you ever tasted ________ kimchee?
Poland	2. We enjoy cooking ________ sausage outside on the grill.
Alaska	3. That restaurant is well known for its ________ crab dishes.
Belgium	4. ________ chocolate is some of the finest in the world.
Sweden	5. One of my favorite dishes is ________ meatballs.
France	6. Sometimes I order my hotdog with ________ fries.
Russia	7. I poured ________ dressing on my salad.
Cuba	8. That restaurant serves the best ________ pork sandwiches.
Peru	9. Have you ever tasted ________ cooking?
India	10. Curry is an ingredient in some ________ dishes.

Name____

40. Understanding Articles

> *A, an,* and *the* point out nouns. They are called **articles.**
>
> GENERAL **St. Louis, Missouri, is a large city.**
>
> PARTICULAR **It is the largest city in Missouri.**

A. Underline each article. Circle the noun each article points out.

1. Long ago St. Louis was a little city near the place where two important rivers came together.
2. People traveled to St. Louis by boat on the Mississippi and Missouri Rivers.
3. These people brought goods to sell to settlers for a profit.
4. A family going west would stop to rest in St. Louis before the big move.
5. An expedition of explorers would stop to get necessary supplies.
6. By the 1840s St. Louis was known as the Gateway to the West.
7. The Mississippi River is still a busy trade route that helps the city grow.
8. Today St. Louis has many railroad lines and a large airport.
9. A vacation in St. Louis is an experience you will not forget.
10. If you take a trip to the city, be sure to visit the Gateway Arch, a reminder of the early pioneer days.

B. Complete each sentence with *a* or *an*.

1. Living in ______ river community like St. Louis can be fun.
2. You can have ______ adventure every week.
3. You can go to ______ hot-air balloon festival in Forest Park.
4. ______ Earth Day parade is also held every year.
5. You can go on ______ steamboat ride on the Mississippi.

Name____________________

41. Using Possessive Adjectives

Possessive adjectives are used before nouns to show possession. These adjectives are *my, your, his, her, its, our,* and *their.*

> **My backpack isn't large enough to hold all those books.**
> **Then you'll have to hold some of them in your arms.**

Circle the correct possessive word in the sentences below.

1. We wouldn't listen to (their theirs) concerns about the high water.

2. One of (my mine) goals had always been to canoe down that stretch of the river.
3. Today (mine my) buddy and I set off with a canoe.
4. There were others at the launch site, strapping on (their theirs) life vests.
5. We put (ours our) vests on, too, and shoved off.
6. We could feel the strong current and had (our ours) doubts about making this trip.
7. As we paddled though, (ours our) fears were replaced by excitement.
8. You can't paddle down that river without (yours your) mind thrilling at the experience.
9. We shot some rapids, and the frothing water nearly ripped (our ours) paddles away from us.
10. In the rapids all (yours your) thoughts must be on dodging rocks and boulders and staying upright.
11. We kept (ours our) craft upright but did take in some water.
12. I thought of my mom; (her hers) biggest fear was that we would capsize.
13. We had no mishaps on (our ours) trip, however.
14. I felt satisfied at having achieved (my mine) goal.
15. In (my mine) buddy's opinion, we should come out and fight the rapids again tomorrow.

Name____

42. Understanding Demonstrative Adjectives

This, that, these, and *those* are **demonstrative adjectives.**
They point out persons, places, or things.
This and *that* point out one person, place, or thing.
These and *those* point out more than one person, place, or thing.
This and *these* point out persons, places, and things that are close.
That and *those* point out persons, places, and things that are far.

ONE, NEAR	**Let's go to this living-history museum.**
MORE THAN ONE, FAR	**I want to see those examples of life in early America.**

Adjectives

A. Underline the demonstrative adjective in each sentence. Write on the line whether it points out one or more than one person, place, or thing.

__________ 1. In this living-history museum people act out the lives of Pilgrims.

__________ 2. We can see what living in that time was like.

__________ 3. The floors of those one-room houses were made of dirt.

__________ 4. Pilgrim women made butter in these churns.

__________ 5. Life is easier in this century, don't you think?

B. Circle the correct demonstrative adjective in parentheses. On the line write if the noun modified is near or far.

__________ 1. In (this those) days Pilgrim children did a lot of work.

__________ 2. The sons helped their fathers in the fields with (these that) tools.

__________ 3. Daughters helped their mothers cook food in (these this) kinds of kettles.

__________ 4. In (those that) period, children didn't have as many toys as they do today.

__________ 5. Would you rather live in (this those) time or way back then?

Name____

43. Using Adjectives to Tell How Many

Some adjectives tell exactly *how many* or *about how many*. These include words such as *ten, thirty, several, few, many,* and *some.*

ABOUT HOW MANY	**Scientists use some measurements to tell about how many.**
EXACTLY HOW MANY	**Rarely do they say exactly how many based on only one guess.**

A. Complete each sentence with an adjective that tells *exactly* or *about* how many. The words at the left will help you choose an adjective.

exactly 1. Twelve inches equals ______________ foot.

about 2. ______________ countries don't use the metric system.

about 3. Touching the wires together caused ______________ sparks.

exactly 4. If I have a dozen eggs, I have exactly ______________ eggs.

about 5. I need a ______________ more inches of copper wire.

about 6. The explosion created ______________ shock waves.

exactly 7. A yard measures ______________ feet.

exactly 8. I need ______________ more quart to make up the gallon.

exactly 9. There are ______________ ounces in one pound.

about 10. The universe probably has ______________ planets.

B. Underline the adjectives. Write on the line whether each adjective tells *exactly how many* or *about how many.*

__________ 1. Seven beakers were lined up.

__________ 2. Some microscopes were delivered.

__________ 3. Several experiments were repeated.

__________ 4. We need five calculators.

__________ 5. Few test tubes are left.

Adjectives

Name____

44. Using Adjectives to Compare

Adjectives can be used to compare two or more persons, places, or things. Many adjectives that end in *-er* compare two nouns. Many adjectives that end in *-est* compare three or more nouns.

Born in 1906, Gertrude Ederle loved to swim as a child.

She swam a greater distance than many adults.

At twelve, she became the youngest person to break a world record.

Other adjectives use *more* to compare two nouns. These same adjectives use *most* to compare three or more nouns.

She was more interested in swimming than anyone she knew.

For Gertrude swimming was the most exciting sport.

Underline the adjective that compares in each sentence.

1. At fourteen, Gertrude swam faster times than fifty-one other women and won an important international swimming event.
2. An even more amazing fact is that Gertrude captured eighteen world swimming records by age seventeen!
3. Gertrude's biggest challenge was swimming across the English Channel.
4. Gertrude's swim of fourteen hours and thirty-one minutes beat the time of the fastest male swimmer by almost two hours.
5. As soon as she stepped out of the water, Gertrude became one of the most admired athletes in the world.

Gertrude Ederle never stopped believing she could reach her goal. Give an example of how you can stay strong and reach your goal.

Name____

45. Working with Adjectives That Compare

Complete each sentence with the correct form of an adjective that compares. Use the adjectives provided in parentheses at the end of each sentence.

1. Goblins may be the ____________________ of all creatures. (creepy)
2. They are ____________________ than trolls. (scary)
3. They are ____________________ than ghosts. (frightening)
4. Their nails are ____________________ than sharks' teeth. (sharp)
5. Goblins shriek ____________________ than a wolf howls. (loud)
6. They are ____________________ than a fox. (crafty)
7. They have the ____________________ smell that you can imagine. (disgusting)
8. Goblins move ____________________ in the shadows than a vampire bat can fly. (fast)
9. They lurk on the roofs of the ____________________ buildings in town. (old)
10. Goblins aren't always found in the ____________________ places. (high)
11. They also hide in gardens in the ____________________ bushes. (thick)
12. Goblins are ____________________ in frightening people than in eating them. (interested)
13. They are the ____________________ of all the creepy creatures. (hungry)
14. Goblins find unicorns even ____________________ than humans. (delicious)
15. At dinner a goblin is ____________________ with roast unicorn. (satisfied)

Name____

46. Using Forms of Good and Bad

Good and *bad* are adjectives. Use *better* or *worse* to compare two things. Use *best* or *worst* to compare three or more things.

GOOD: TWO THINGS	**The weather is better today than yesterday.**
GOOD: THREE OR MORE THINGS	**This is the best weather we have had all month.**
BAD: TWO THINGS	**This storm is worse than last month's storm.**
BAD: THREE OR MORE THINGS	**This storm is the worst I have ever seen.**

Adjectives

Choose the correct adjective to complete each sentence.

good better best

1. People have always wanted to control the climate and make their weather ________ than before.
2. One ________ solution is to live where you already like the climate.
3. Many people can't move to a ________ climate, so they just try their best to feel more comfortable where they are.
4. In hot climates it is a ________ idea to wear light clothes and stay in the shade.
5. In very hot climates the ________ solution is air conditioning!

bad worse worst

6. Living in a ________ climate can make life uncomfortable.
7. Heavy rains can make driving conditions ________ than before.
8. Very high temperatures create ________ conditions for plants, animals, and people.
9. Heavy snow and ice may be the ________ conditions of all.
10. Most people think a frigid climate is ________ than a tropical climate.

Name ____

47. Reviewing Adjectives

A. Complete each sentence with *a, an,* or *the.* Circle the proper adjective in each sentence.

1. California has _____ large number of people of Mexican ancestry.
2. It also has one of _____ largest Chinese communities outside Asia.
3. _____ English sea captain Sir Francis Drake claimed California for England.
4. California was under _____ Spanish flag at one point in history.
5. It became _____ American state in 1850.

B. Complete each sentence with *this, that, these,* or *those.* The words at the left will help you choose the adjective.

one, near	1. ________ state seal is for California.
more than one, far	2. ________ pictures show gold ore.
one, far	3. ________ bird, the California Valley Quail, has become the state bird.
more than one, near	4. ________ redwood trees are magnificent.
one, near	5. ________ part of the coast is my favorite.

C. Complete each sentence with an adjective that tells *exactly how many* or *about how many.* The words at the left will help you choose an adjective.

about	1. ____________ people came to California to find gold.
exactly	2. There is only ____________ film capital of the world—Hollywood!
about	3. In 1906 a big earthquake destroyed ____________ buildings.
about	4. Disneyland has ____________ kinds of rides.
exactly	5. California had ____________ state capitals before Sacramento—San José, Vallejo, and Benicia.

Name____

D. Complete each sentence with the correct form of the adjective at the left.

large	1. California is one of the __________ producers of manufactured goods.
popular	2. The Golden Gate Bridge is one of the __________ symbols of the state of California.
bad	3. The air pollution in Los Angeles is __________ than it is in Sacramento.
beautiful	4. Do you think the mountains or the beaches are __________?
good	5. The __________ vacation I ever had was my trip to California.

Try It Yourself

What do you know about your state? Write four sentences describing things you like about it, using adjectives.

____

____

____

____

Check Your Own Work

Choose a piece of writing from your portfolio, a work in progress, an assignment from another class, or a letter. Revise it, using the skills you have reviewed. The checklist will help you.

- ✔ Have you chosen adjectives that paint a clear picture?
- ✔ Have you used articles correctly?
- ✔ Have you chosen the correct form of the adjectives for comparison?

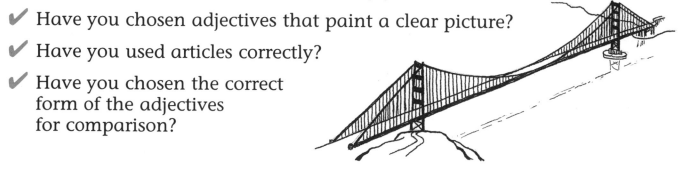

Name ____________________

48. Identifying Action Verbs

Many verbs express action. **Action verbs** tell what someone or something does.

Our body parts perform many different jobs.

A. Underline the action verb(s) in each sentence.

1. The nose cleans the air we take in.
2. The diaphragm forces air in and out of our lungs.
3. The vibration of our vocal cords produces sound.
4. The heart pumps blood throughout the body.
5. Blood carries oxygen and nutrients to all parts of the body.
6. It also fights infections and helps clots form.
7. Our skin also protects us from germs and infection.
8. Kidneys clean and filter our blood.
9. Tears from tear ducts wash and clean our eyes.
10. Our teeth break food into small pieces for digestion.

B. Look at the action verbs listed. Choose the one that completes each sentence and write it on the line. Check to see if you need a singular or plural form.

cool **control** **support** **prevent** **store**

1. Our eyelashes ________ particles from hurting our eyes.
2. Our bones ________ our bodies.
3. The inner ear ________ our balance.
4. Sweat glands ________ our bodies when we are too hot.
5. The fat cells of our bodies ________ energy.

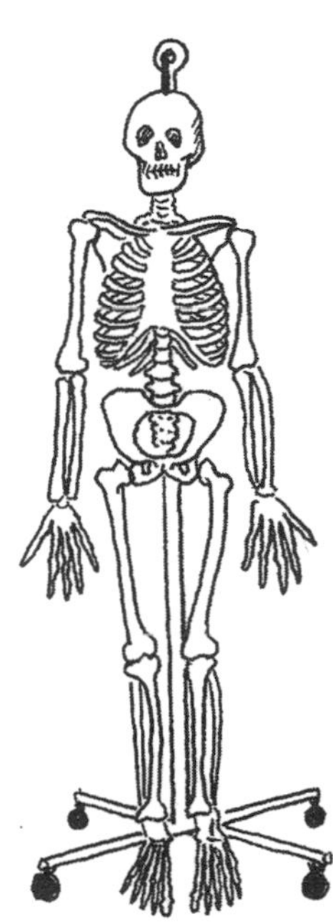

Name ____________________

49. Working with Action Verbs

A. Complete each sentence with an action verb. Choose from the action verbs below. Each verb is used only once.

wish	**tastes**	**drink**	**spread**	**eat**
pour	**makes**	**buy**	**cuts**	**toasts**

1. Many people ________ milk at breakfast.
2. Sometimes they ________ it over their cereal.
3. It also ________ good in coffee or tea.
4. We ________ a gallon of milk at the grocery store every week.
5. For lunch we drink juice and ________ sandwiches.
6. My mother ________ a sandwich for me every day.
7. She ________ the bread.
8. I watch her ________ the peanut butter and jelly on it.
9. Then she ________ the sandwich into four triangles.
10. My friends ________ their moms made their lunches for them.

B. What actions can you do with the following objects? Write the action verb on the line.

soap	1. ____________	towel	6. ____________
pen	2. ____________	book	7. ____________
oven	3. ____________	crayon	8. ____________
knife	4. ____________	tea kettle	9. ____________
ball	5. ____________	piano	10. ____________

Verbs

Name____

50. Identifying Being Verbs

A **being verb** shows what someone or something is. Being verbs do not express action. Some being verbs are *am, is, are, was, were, has been, had been, have been,* and *will be.*

There are many surprising special effects in space.

A. Circle the being verb in each sentence.

1. One special effect is a solar flare.
2. These bright flashes of light from the sun are electromagnetic radiation.
3. Another special effect is an eclipse.
4. There have been sightings of eclipses for centuries.
5. In a lunar eclipse, the moon is in Earth's shadow.
6. In a solar eclipse, Earth is in the moon's shadow.
7. In either case, the result will be a large, dark circle in the sky.
8. The best special effects are auroras.
9. Auroras have been around for millions of years.
10. They are beautiful curtains of colored lights in the sky.

B. Underline the verb in each sentence. Write on the line A when the verb expresses action and B when the verb expresses being.

_____ 1. Another special effect from space is a comet.

_____ 2. Comets are collections of minerals, dust, gases, and ice particles.

_____ 3. Their glowing tails of dust, gas, and reflected sunlight can be millions of miles long.

_____ 4. Comets travel in orbits and in regular cycles.

_____ 5. For example, Halley's comet returns every seventy-six years.

Name____

51. Identifying Linking Verbs

A **linking verb** is often a being verb. A linking verb joins the subject of a sentence to a noun, a pronoun, or an adjective. Some linking verbs are *am, is, are, was, were, has been, have been, had been,* and *will be.*

A. Underline the linking verb in each sentence.

1. My father has been a birdwatcher for many years.
2. It was he who took me on my first trip to watch birds.
3. Our location for watching was a beautiful redwood forest.
4. After we had been quiet for a long time, we saw it!
5. It was a northern spotted owl.

Verbs

B. Write on the line whether the *italicized* word is a noun, a pronoun, or an adjective. Underline the subject to which it is linked.

__________ 1. Many birds are *small.*

__________ 2. One of the biggest birds is the *emu.*

__________ 3. It is very *fast* and can run 30 miles per hour.

__________ 4. At one point the emu was almost *extinct.*

__________ 5. Now there are more emus; these birds are *survivors.*

C. Complete each sentence with a linking verb.

1. Birds ______________ the only animals covered with feathers.
2. There ______________ about 9,000 types of birds on the planet.
3. The fastest bird ______________ the white-throated spinetail swift.
4. Some scientists think birds and dinosaurs ______________ members of the same family a long time ago.
5. One day the answer to this question ______________ clear.

Name____

52. Identifying Helping Verbs

A **helping verb** is always followed by another verb. Some helping verbs are *am, is, are, was, were, be, being, been, shall, will, may, can, has, have, had, do, does, did, should, would, could,* and *must.*

At one time tulips were bought and sold like jewels.

A. The verb is *italicized* in each sentence. Write **LV** on the line if the verb in the sentence is a linking verb or **HV** if it is a helping verb.

_____ 1. "Tulipmania" *was* an obsession and a way to make a lot of money.

_____ 2. In Holland, between 1634 and 1637, people *were* selling tulips for huge amounts of money.

_____ 3. Rich people from many countries *were* anxious to collect the rarest and most unusual tulips.

_____ 4. A document *has been* found that shows a man paid thousands of dollars' worth of animals, wine, beer, butter, cheese, furniture, clothes, and silver for ONE single tulip bulb!

_____ 5. After a while people got tired of tulips; they *had been* just another fad.

B. Circle the linking verb or underline the helping verb in each sentence.

1. The agave plant has grown in Mexico for centuries.
2. It is a very useful plant.
3. Long ago people would use agave fibers as thread.
4. They could make a kind of needle from its sharp points.
5. Different parts of the plant were a source of food and drink.

Name____

53. Understanding Verbs and Sentences

The verb is the most important word in a sentence. Without a verb, there is no sentence, only a sentence fragment. Sometimes a verb is the only word in a sentence.

SENTENCE	**Look!**
SENTENCE	**The whales are surfacing!**
SENTENCE FRAGMENT	**The whales**

Read each group of words. Write S on the line if the group of words is a sentence or NS if it is not a sentence. Put a period after the sentence.

_____ 1. Whales are amazing creatures

_____ 2. In the water

_____ 3. There are no freshwater whales

_____ 4. Sleek smooth skin

_____ 5. A thick layer of blubber insulates them from the cold

_____ 6. The blowhole, or nose, is at the top of the head

_____ 7. Some whales feed on plankton

_____ 8. The gray whale and the rorqual whale

_____ 9. Other whales feed on fish and squid

_____ 10. The sperm whale and the narwhal whale are of this type

_____ 11. Sperm whales from 1 to 3 kilometers deep

_____ 12. Whales were and are hunted for their meat and oil

_____ 13. Environmental groups

_____ 14. Many species of whales face extinction

_____ 15. Fifty-million-year-old whale fossil in Pakistan

Name____

54. Recognizing Verb Phrases

A **verb phrase** is made up of one or more helping verbs and a main verb.

HELPING VERB	**People have listened to stories for centuries.**
MAIN VERB	**People have listened to stories for centuries.**
VERB PHRASE	**People have listened to stories for centuries.**

A. Underline the verb phrase in each sentence. Circle the main verb.

1. Stories have always been told all around the world.
2. Stories have been used for different purposes.
3. They can teach us admirable behavior.
4. They can entertain us.
5. They can remind us of the past.
6. In most societies different kinds of stories are told.
7. Children have always enjoyed the adventures in fairy tales.
8. Other tales, called fables, have taught correct behavior through the moral of the story.
9. In pioneer days tall tales were created about extraordinary people and their impossible feats.
10. These funny stories would make people feel better during difficult times.

Fairy Tales

TALL TALES

FABLES

B. Complete each sentence with a helping verb. Two blank lines mean that two helping verbs are needed.

1. In tall tales people ______________ step over mountains and drink up rivers!
2. Children know they ______________ hear a fairy tale when the storyteller begins with "Once upon a time."
3. Animals ______________ always been the main characters in fables.
4. ______________ you ______________ reading any new stories?
5. If you tell me a story, then I ______________ tell you one!

Name____________________

55. Identifying Regular and Irregular Verbs

There are four principal parts of a verb—**present**, present participle, **past**, and past participle.

The **present participle** is formed by adding *-ing* to the present form of the verb. The present participle is used with a form of the verb *be*, such as *is, are, was,* or *were.*

The **past participle** of a regular verb is formed by adding *-d* or *-ed* to the present. The past participle of an irregular verb is not formed by adding *-d* or *-ed* to the present. The past participle is used with a helping verb such as *has, have,* or *had.*

	Present	Present participle	Past	Past participle
Regular Verb	**bake**	is **baking**	**baked**	**(has, have, had) baked**
Irregular Verb	**swim**	is **swimming**	**swam**	**(has, have, had) swum**

A. Write on the line the principal part (present, present participle, past, or past participle) of the *italicized* verb in each sentence.

________ 1. My family always has *liked* sports.

________ 2. My mother *learned* to swim at an early age.

________ 3. My father is *playing* in a golf tournament.

________ 4. My brothers *love* to play soccer.

________ 5. I have always *enjoyed* tennis.

B. Write **R** on the line if the *italicized* verb is regular or **I** if it is irregular.

____ 1. Sports *are* a wonderful form of exercise.

____ 2. They *increase* muscular strength.

____ 3. They *have* other benefits too.

____ 4. You *make* friends easily when you play a sport.

____ 5. What new sport are you *trying*?

Name____

56. Working with Irregular Verbs

A. Complete each sentence with the past or past participle form of the irregular verb shown at the left.

write 1. Many authors have ________ about the Wright brothers.

go 2. I ________ to the library to check out a book about their lives.

be 3. The Wright brothers had ________ obsessed with the idea of flight.

draw 4. They ________ many different designs for flying machines, some with engines and some without.

build 5. Orville and Wilbur Wright also ________ an early version of the wind tunnel.

fly 6. On his first flight Orville Wright had ________ for twelve seconds.

make 7. Orville and Wilbur ________ three more flights.

spend 8. In 1906 the Wright brothers had ________ more than an hour in the air on one flight.

grow 9. Interest in flying machines ________ quickly.

begin 10. By 1910 the Wright brothers had ________ their own company, called the American Wright Company.

B. Write in the chart the missing form of each irregular verb.

Base Form of Verb	Past	Past Participle
1. blow	________	blown
2. come	came	________
3. ________	chose	chosen
4. do	did	________
5. eat	________	eaten
6. hide	hid	________
7. ________	knew	known
8. leave	left	________
9. meet	________	met
10. pay	________	paid

Verbs

Name____

57. Using Begin, Beginning, Began, Begun

The principal parts of *begin* are as follows:

Present	Present Participle	Past	Past Participle
begin	**beginning**	**began**	**begun**

The present participle is always used with a helping verb such as *is, are, was,* or *were.*
The past participle is always used with a helping verb such as *has, have,* or *had.*

Complete each story with *beginning, began,* or *begun.* Then guess whom or what the story is about. Use the names listed to help you.

Great Chicago Fire **John Wilkes Booth** **Mount Vesuvius**
the *Titanic* **Boston Tea Party**

1. The iceberg that the ship hit was huge. The ship ________ to sink as water rushed in. People had ________ fighting for the lifeboats. ______________
2. The theater was full, because President Lincoln was there. The play was ________. When they heard the shot, people ________ to scream. ______________
3. Smoke had ________ to come out of the top of the mountain a few weeks before. Fire, ash, and lava ________ to rain down. People and animals were trapped in their houses. ______________
4. Mrs. O'Leary's cow may have kicked over the lantern. Flames were ________ to spread out of the barn. The city's biggest disaster had ________. ______________
5. The patriots, masquerading as Mohawk Indians, boarded the ships. They ________ throwing chests of tea into the harbor. A rebellion had ________.

____

Verbs

Name ____________________

58. Using Break, Breaking, Broke, Broken; Choose, Choosing, Chose, Chosen

The principal parts of *break* and *choose* are as follows:

Present	Present Participle	Past	Past Participle
break	**breaking**	**broke**	**broken**
choose	**choosing**	**chose**	**chosen**

The present participle is always used with a helping verb such as *is, are, was,* or *were.*
The past participle is always used with a helping verb such as *has, have,* or *had.*

A. Complete each sentence with *break, breaking, broke,* or *broken.*

1. The secret agent ____________ the seal of the envelope containing his instructions.
2. He was ____________ into enemy headquarters.
3. He needed to find out if the enemy had ____________ the secret code.
4. Spies ____________ secret codes all the time.
5. The enemy ____________ the secret code just minutes before the agent arrived.

B. Complete each sentence with *choose, choosing, chose,* or *chosen.*

1. How do people ____________ friends?
2. Some people have ____________ friends because they are interested in the same things.
3. Some people have friends because someone ____________ them!
4. When I am ____________ a friend, I look for someone who makes me laugh.
5. I am lucky you ____________ me as your friend.

Name____

59. Using Do, Doing, Did, Done

The principal parts of *do* are as follows:

Present	Present Participle	Past	Past Participle
do	**doing**	**did**	**done**

The present participle is always used with a helping verb such as *is, are, was,* or *were.*
The past participle is always used with a helping verb such as *has, have,* or *had.*

Complete each sentence with *do, doing, did,* or *done.*

People often remember childhood songs, poems, and stories. One favorite story is *Miss Nelson Is Missing*.

Miss Nelson was a very sweet and patient teacher. Her students were not so sweet. They were ______ (1) many bad things in class. They never ______ (2) their work. Miss Nelson wondered what to ______ (3). Then she knew.

The next day Miss Nelson's students had a new teacher. She wasn't sweet OR patient. "What? You haven't ______ (4) your work? What will I ______ (5) with you?" she would say.

Many days passed. Now the students always ______ (6) their homework. They were ______ (7) everything the teacher wanted them to ______ (8). They had not ______ (9) anything bad in a long time. (Or anything fun, either!)

One day Miss Nelson came back. "Oh," said the students, "we missed you so much!"

"______ (10) you?" said Miss Nelson, looking very happy.

Verbs

Name____

60. Reviewing Regular and Irregular Verbs

A. Underline the regular verb or verb phrase in each sentence. Draw a circle around the irregular verb or verb phrase in each sentence.

1. We have seen a forest fire on the TV news.
2. We look at the images of black, broken trees.
3. Can nature survive after such a terrible fire?
4. Strangely, fires can actually help forests.
5. The forest floor fills with the dead branches of bushes and plants.
6. Then new trees do not have enough room.
7. Fires change the dead material into soil-enriching ash.
8. The trees can get necessary nutrients from this ash.
9. New trees grow in this rich soil.
10. Eventually the forest is green and healthy looking again.

B. Underline the verb or verb phrase in each sentence. Write on the line the form the underlined main verb is in.

What do you know about redwood trees? ____present____

1. Some redwood trees can live more than 2,000 years. ______________
2. Chemicals in the wood have made them resistant to many diseases and insects. ______________
3. Some redwoods have grown to be taller than the Statue of Liberty! ______________
4. The diameters of some redwood trunks are from ten to fifteen feet. ______________
5. We were actually driving a car through a hole in the trunk of a famous redwood tree in California! ______________

Name____

61. Understanding Simple Tenses

There are three simple tenses.
The **simple present** tells about an action that happens again and again. The **simple past** tells about an action that happened in the past. The **simple future tense** tells about an action that will happen in the future. The helping verb *will* is used to form the future tense.

PRESENT	**Our dog follows me to school every day.**
PAST	**Yesterday the neighbor's dog followed me too.**
FUTURE	**How many dogs will follow me tomorrow?**

A. **Circle the correct form of the present tense of each verb in parentheses.**

1. Baboons (bite bites) only their attackers.
2. An armadillo (curl curls) up inside its shell when frightened.
3. Whales (push pushes) their powerful tails up and down to swim.
4. Dolphins (jump jumps) into the air during aquatic shows.
5. Trained lions (allow allows) their trainers to get in their cages with them.
6. A pet myna bird (pronounce pronounces) words its owner teaches it.
7. Many snakes (hide hides) from rather than attack people coming too close.
8. Monkeys (warn warns) people to stand still by showing their teeth.
9. A wild bird like the falcon (accept accepts) training by humans.
10. Animals (is are) not always so fierce as we imagine.

B. **Read each sentence carefully. Circle the correct past or future form of each verb.**

1. When my friend arrives, I (will go went) to the pet store to buy a pet.
2. I (will have had) a hamster before, but now I want a cat.
3. My mother says a cat (will make made) a great pet.
4. She (will own owned) a cat when she was a child.
5. I (will enjoy enjoyed) playing with a soft, furry cat tomorrow.

Verbs

Name____

62. Working with Simple Tenses

> A verb can be in the simple present, the simple past, or the simple future tense.

A. **Write on the line whether the *italicized* verb in each sentence is in the present, past, or future.**

__________ 1. Sea otters *are* fascinating animals.

__________ 2. Sea otters *sleep* in the sea.

__________ 3. A sea otter *will wrap* kelp around its body.

__________ 4. The seaweed *keeps* the otter in one place as it sleeps.

__________ 5. I *saw* a sea otter do a very clever thing.

__________ 6. The sea otter *floated* on its back at mealtime.

__________ 7. It *used* its belly as a table!

__________ 8. In general, a sea otter *eats* abalone, clams, and crabs.

__________ 9. It *will crush* the shell of a clam, crab, or mussel with its powerful teeth.

__________ 10. Sea otters *remain* playful animals, even when adult.

B. **Complete each sentence with the correct verb form. The verb and the tense are indicated in parentheses.**

(belong—present) 1. Beavers __________ to the rodent family.

(have—present) 2. They __________ waterproof coats and powerful legs.

(weigh—future) 3. Beavers __________ up to 100 pounds on occasion.

(see—past) 4. My class and I __________ a family of beavers construct a lodge.

(build—past) 5. They __________ a home that was more than 20 feet wide!

Verbs

Name____

63. Identifying the Present Progressive Tense

The **present progressive tense** tells what is happening now. The present progressive tense is formed with the present participle and a present form of the verb be (*am, is,* or *are*).

PRESENT PARTICIPLE	**They are going to the zoo by bus.**
PRESENT FORM OF *BE*	**They are going to the zoo by bus.**
PRESENT PROGRESSIVE TENSE	**They are going to the zoo by bus.**

Complete each sentence by forming the present progressive tense of the verbs in parentheses.

1. My mother ____________________ me to the zoo. (drive)
2. I ____________________ my camera. (bring)
3. I ____________________ my friends by the ape house. (meet)
4. They ____________________ the newborn gorilla. (watch)
5. The newborn calf ____________________ right now. (feed)
6. We ____________________ to the large mammal house after this. (go)
7. Elephants and giraffes ____________________ just feet from us. (stand)
8. People ____________________ peanuts to the elephants. (throw)
9. The giraffe ____________________ for my camera. (pose)
10. I ____________________ a picture of an extremely tall animal. (take)
11. My friends and I ____________________ the seals next. (see)
12. The seals ____________________ around in circles. (swim)
13. They ____________________ fish from the zookeeper. (eat)
14. We ____________________ at the noises the seals make. (laugh)
15. We ____________________ the zoo soon. (leave)

Name____

64. Identifying the Past Progressive Tense

The **past progressive tense** tells what was happening in the past. The past progressive tense is formed with the present participle and a past form of the verb *be* (*was* and *were*).

PRESENT PARTICIPLE	**She was petting the dog.**
PAST FORM OF *BE*	**She was petting the dog.**
PAST PROGRESSIVE TENSE	**She was petting the dog.**

Complete each sentence by forming the past progressive tense of the verbs in parentheses.

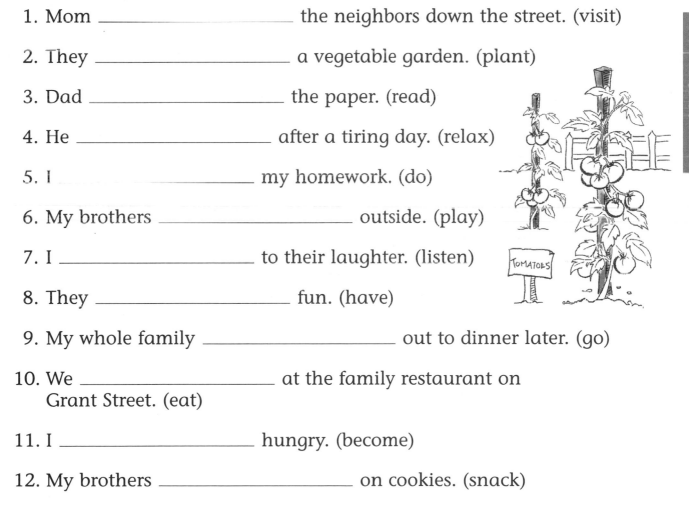

1. Mom ______________________ the neighbors down the street. (visit)
2. They ______________________ a vegetable garden. (plant)
3. Dad ______________________ the paper. (read)
4. He ______________________ after a tiring day. (relax)
5. I ______________________ my homework. (do)
6. My brothers ______________________ outside. (play)
7. I ______________________ to their laughter. (listen)
8. They ______________________ fun. (have)
9. My whole family ______________________ out to dinner later. (go)
10. We ______________________ at the family restaurant on Grant Street. (eat)
11. I ______________________ hungry. (become)
12. My brothers ______________________ on cookies. (snack)
13. They ______________________ their appetites for dinner. (ruin)
14. It ______________________ by dinnertime. (rain)
15. We ______________________ to the restaurant. (drive)

Name________________________________

65. Understanding Subject and Verb Agreement: Is, Am, Are, Was, Were

A subject and a verb must always **agree**. A singular subject must have a singular verb. *Is, am,* and *was* are singular verbs. A plural subject must have a plural verb. *Are* and *were* are plural verbs. When the pronoun *you* is the subject, *are* or *were* is used, because *you* always takes a plural verb.

A. Complete each sentence with *is, am,* or *are.*

1. Did you know that chocolate ________ made from beans?
2. These beans ________ from the cacao plant.
3. The sugar and fat in chocolate ________ a source of energy.
4. I ________ crazy about chocolate.
5. ________ chocolate one of your favorite foods too?

B. Complete each sentence with *was* or *were.*

1. The cacao plant ________ known to Indians in Central and South America over 4,000 years ago.
2. Back then, chocolate ________ a drink, not a candy.
3. Samples of chocolate and cacao beans ________ brought back to Europe by Hernán Cortés, the Spanish explorer.
4. Europeans ________ soon happily drinking chocolate.
5. It ________ in the 1800s when a Dutch scientist learned how to make chocolate into candy.

C. Complete the sentences with *is, am, are, was,* or *were.*

1. For a good dessert, get some strawberries that ________ red and ripe.
2. After they ________ washed, heat some chocolate in a pot.
3. When the chocolate ________ soft and warm, dip the strawberries into it.
4. Wait until the chocolate ________ cool, then eat and enjoy!
5. Now that ________ easy, don't you think?

Name____

66. Understanding Subject and Verb Agreement: Do and Does

Does is a singular verb. *Do* is a plural verb but is also used with *I* and *you*.

Does your teacher explain the value of good study habits?
Good students do several important things before they study.
Do you have good study habits?

A. Complete each sentence with *does* or *do*.

1. Some students ________ their homework promptly.
2. They often ________ a lot of reading or research.
3. My brother ________ his homework every day.
4. He ________ best in math and science.
5. I ________ best in art and music!

B. Circle the correct verb form.

1. Many students (do does) extra reading.
2. They (do does) their assignments promptly.
3. She (do does) research in the library.
4. She also (do does) research on the computer at home.
5. My brother (do does) physical exercise before homework.
6. My sisters (do does) their exercising after their homework is finished.
7. Many students (do does) not like homework.
8. They are afraid they won't (do does) well on it.
9. Most of the time they (do does) just fine.
10. (Do Does) you have homework tonight?

Name____

67. Using There Is and There Are

When a sentence starts with *there is* or *there are,* the subject of the sentence follows the verb.

There is a waiting list for the swimming class.
(*Waiting list* is the subject. It follows the verb *is.*)

There are many people on the waiting list.
(*People* is the subject. It follows the verb *are.*)

A. Circle the subject that follows the verb *is* or *are.* Write **S** on the line if the subject and verb are singular or **P** if they are plural.

_____ 1. There are many objects in our solar system.

_____ 2. There is only one sun.

_____ 3. There are nine major planets that orbit the sun.

_____ 4. There are moons that orbit seven of the planets.

_____ 5. There are two planets with no moons—Mercury and Venus.

_____ 6. There are two planets you can't see with your eyes—Neptune and Pluto.

_____ 7. There are other things, such as asteroids and meteoroids, in the solar system.

_____ 8. There is a special phenomenon called the solar wind.

_____ 9. There are many comets with long, dusty tails.

_____ 10. There is mostly just empty space, however.

B. Underline the subject that follows the verb in each sentence. Circle the correct verb in parentheses.

1. Long ago there (was were) strange ideas about the solar system.
2. There (was were) a man named Ptolemy who said Earth didn't move and that other parts of the solar system revolved around Earth.
3. There (was were) people who said Earth rested on a giant turtle.
4. There (was were) a belief that a giant dog took bites out of the moon during an eclipse.
5. There (was were) a society that believed Earth was flat.

Name____

68. Reviewing Verbs

A. Write **A** on the line if the *italicized* verb in each sentence is an action verb or **B** if it is a being verb.

_____ 1. Sculptors *are* artists who make monuments and statues.

_____ 2. These monuments and statues *help* us remember special people or important events in history.

_____ 3. Communities often *ask* sculptors to create big, important works to display in front of city buildings.

_____ 4. People *visit* a monument or statue and think about the person or event it pictures.

_____ 5. The monument or statue *is* a way to show respect for the past.

B. Underline the helping verb in each sentence. Circle the main verb.

1. Many monuments and statues are created as war memorials.
2. All around the United States, sculptors have made memorials for different wars.
3. One of the most famous memorials was installed in Washington, D.C.
4. A 21-year-old woman named Maya Lin had designed it.
5. This memorial has been known as the Vietnam Veterans Memorial.

C. Write **R** on the line if the *italicized* verb is regular or **I** if it is irregular.

_____ 1. Maya Lin *grew* up in Athens, Ohio, and finished high school there with excellent grades.

_____ 2. She was *accepted* to Yale University as an architecture student.

_____ 3. When she was a senior at Yale, she *heard* about the contest to design a monument to honor the soldiers who fought in Vietnam.

_____ 4. Many people were surprised that a young Chinese-American woman had *won* the contest to design the memorial.

_____ 5. Many other people didn't *like* her design.

CONTINUED

Name____

D. Circle **N** if the *italicized* word is a noun and **A** if it is an adjective.

N A 1. Maya Lin's design was a plain V-shaped *wall*.

N A 2. All the stone of the wall was *black*.

N A 3. The carving on the wall was not *decorative*.

N A 4. It was a simple *list* of the 58,000 people who had died in the war.

N A 5. Maya Lin was very *upset* about the criticism of her project.

Maya Lin continued to work hard even when people didn't like her ideas. Give an example of when it is important not to give up.

Try It Yourself

If you were to build a monument or statue, whom or what would it be for? Why? What would it look like? Write four sentences about these things. Be sure to use action and being verbs and to use helping verbs where necessary.

____

____

____

____

Check Your Own Work

Choose a piece of writing from your portfolio, a work in progress, an assignment from another class, or a letter. Revise it, using the skills you have reviewed. The checklist will help you.

✔ Have you formed the principal parts of your regular and irregular verbs correctly?

✔ Have you used the correct tenses of verbs in your sentences?

✔ Do all of your subjects and verbs agree?

Name ______________________________

69. Identifying Adverbs of Time

An **adverb** modifies a verb, an adjective, or another adverb. An adverb tells *when, where,* or *how.* **Adverbs of time** answer the questions *when* or *how often.* Some adverbs of time are *again, always, early, immediately, now, often, sometimes, soon, then, today, tomorrow,* and *yesterday.*

WHEN? **I will return the library book tomorrow.**
HOW OFTEN? **I often reread favorite books.**

A. Circle the adverbs that tell when or how often.

1. I will always remember the movie *Where the Red Fern Grows.*
2. Yesterday I went to the library for the book of the same title.
3. I found it immediately and began reading about Billy, the main character.
4. Billy frequently dreamed of owning his own hounds.
5. Early in the day he found a magazine with an ad for dogs.
6. First he had to save the money he needed.
7. Billy sometimes walked in the woods to help him think.
8. He often walked by a camp as he followed raccoon tracks.
9. He wondered again about buying the dogs.
10. Could he ever save fifty dollars?

B. Complete each sentence with an adverb of time from the list. Use each word once.

daily **finally** **frequently** **never** **tomorrow**

1. Billy worked ________ to earn the money for the hounds.
2. ________, probably five times a week, he thought about the dogs.
3. Billy ________ bought candy while he was saving his money.
4. ________ the happy day arrived.
5. ________ Billy would chase raccoons with his two pups.

Name____

70. Identifying Adverbs of Place

Adverbs of place answer the question *where*. Some adverbs of place are *above, away, back, below, down, everywhere, far, forward, here, in, inside, near, outside, there, up,* and *within*.

WHERE? **She had to go in just as the boys did.**
What she saw inside really pleased her.

Circle the adverb that tells where in each sentence.

1. We drove inside, to the photo safari grounds.
2. We could see different animals everywhere we looked!
3. There, in the trees, were at least three kinds of monkeys.
4. We could see an orangutan climbing up.
5. He began picking fruit and throwing it down to the ground.
6. We saw a large snake nearby, winding itself into a coil.
7. We stepped back to take photos of a pair of lions.
8. Some small antelope jumped forward as we approached them.
9. Colorful, noisy birds flew above as we drove by.
10. Some zebras moved away, trying to avoid us.
11. The kangaroo turned sideways and wouldn't let us photograph her.
12. We watched the kangaroo's pouch to see if there was a baby within.
13. We did get good pictures of a giraffe at a water hole outside.
14. We couldn't find an ostrich anywhere.
15. The whole family agreed to come here again next year.

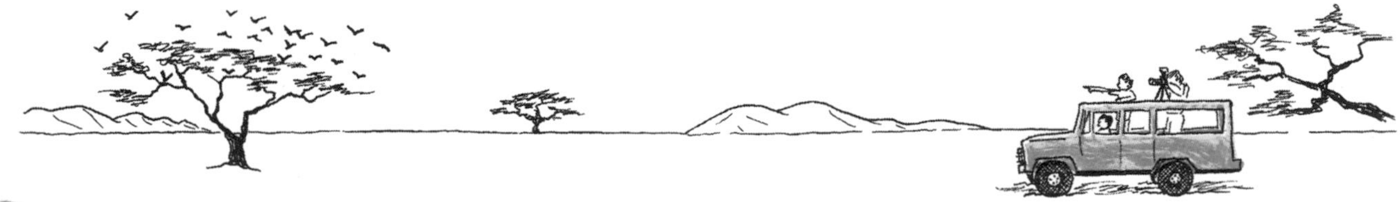

Name____

71. Identifying Adverbs of Manner

Adverbs of manner answer the question *how*. Some adverbs of manner are *carefully, clearly, easily, gracefully, happily, kindly, quickly,* and *slowly*. Many adverbs end in *-ly,* but some, such as *fast, well,* and *hard,* do not.

How? **The science teacher closed the door quietly.**
She looked at the students quickly.

A. Circle the adverb that tells how in each sentence.

1. The students in the science lab were not working silently.
2. At table one, students yelled excitedly as two insects raced each other.
3. At table two, Roberto was carefully trying to stack three beakers.
4. At table three, students clapped each time the turtle curiously poked its head out of its shell.
5. At table four, Sarah and Hyun Jung were loudly reciting the names of elements from the periodic table.
6. At table five, Joanna was dreamily singing along to her headset.
7. At table six, Carl and Jack were happily tossing the globe of the world back and forth.
8. At table seven, students counted patiently to see how long Jaehak could hold his breath.
9. At table eight, Butch was slowly pouring ink all over the science projects.
10. The new teacher awoke suddenly—it had all been just a bad dream!

B. Complete each sentence with an adverb of manner. Use each word once.

attentively **neatly** **politely** **regularly** **well**

1. In order to do __________ in school, it is important to have good study habits.
2. Always listen __________ to the teacher.
3. Listen and then take notes __________ so that you can read them later on.
4. Raise your hand __________ to clarify something or ask a question.
5. Review your class notes and assignments __________.

Adverbs

Name____

72. Recognizing Kinds of Adverbs

An adverb modifies a verb, an adjective, or another adverb. There are adverbs of time *(when?)*, place *(where?)*, and manner *(how?)*.

adverb of time (when?)	**The class visited Aqua World yesterday.**
adverb of place (where?)	**They want to go there again.**
adverb of manner (how?)	**They left Aqua World reluctantly.**

A. List each adverb in the correct column.

backward	**early**	**forward**	**immediately**	**someday**
cautiously	**everywhere**	**gracefully**	**nearby**	**suddenly**
curiously	**expertly**	**inside**	**silently**	**weekly**

TIME	PLACE	MANNER
1. ____________	6. ____________	11. ____________
2. ____________	7. ____________	12. ____________
3. ____________	8. ____________	13. ____________
4. ____________	9. ____________	14. ____________
5. ____________	10. ____________	15. ____________

B. Complete each sentence with an appropriate adverb from the list.

1. The students ____________ approached the underground glass wall.
2. Lateesha stared ____________ into the water behind the glass wall.
3. Hundreds of fish swam ____________ in the deep blue depths.
4. ____________ she saw a huge gray shark.
5. It circled the tank slowly and then swam ____________, where she stood.
6. Lateesha involuntarily stepped ____________ when she saw its many teeth.
7. Goosebumps appeared ____________ on her arms!
8. Next, she saw an octopus propel itself ____________, toward the glass wall.
9. Then, a huge eel left its hiding place ____________.
10. What scary but fascinating creatures to visit again ____________!

Adverbs

Name____

73. Comparing with Adverbs

Like adjectives, many adverbs can be used to make comparisons. Adverbs compare the actions of two or more persons, places, or things. Some adverbs end in *-ier* or *-iest* and others are used with *more* and *most.*

-IER	**Peter gets up to lift weights earlier than Tom.**
-IEST	**Of the three, Francisco gets up earliest to lift weights.**
MORE	**Sandra swims laps more often than Gloria.**
MOST	**Of the three Julia swims laps most often.**

A. Underline the adverb that compares in each sentence. Write on the line whether the adverb is an adverb of time, place, or manner.

__________ 1. Sidney works out more regularly than John does.

__________ 2. In the vaulting competition, Mike jumped highest.

__________ 3. The team is starting the season later than usual.

__________ 4. Helena dives more expertly than Greta.

__________ 5. This year's relay team runs faster than last year's team.

Adverbs

B. Circle the correct form of the adverb in parentheses.

1. Mary Lou runs (more gracefully gracefully) than Sue does.
2. Frank plays basketball (skillfully most skillfully) of all the players.
3. Geraldo works really (harder hard) at the parallel bars.
4. We play soccer (more frequently frequently) than they do.
5. Jorge arrived at the finish line (soon sooner) than Charles.

C. Complete each sentence with an appropriate adverb from the list. Use the correct form of each adverb. Use each adverb once.

accurately aggressively fast often regularly

1. Our baseball team is losing ______________ than usual these days.
2. Selena runs ______________ of all the members of the track team.
3. Juan is pitching ______________ than he did last year.
4. They play tennis ______________ every week.
5. The hockey team is playing ______________ than usual.

Name____

74. Using Good and Well; No, Not, and Never

The word *good* is an adjective. The word *well* is an adverb.

ADVERB **Are you doing well in school?**

ADJECTIVE **Yes, my grades are good.**

Use only one negative word in a sentence to express a negative idea.

What? You do not have any bad grades?
I have never had bad grades!

A. Complete each sentence with *good* or *well.*

1. Can he do this job ________?
   I'm sure he can. He is a ________ worker.
2. The new violinist is quite ________.
   I agree. He has been playing very ________ all night.
3. Grapes grow ________ in hot, dry climates.
   I know. California grapes make really ________ jam!
4. This knife doesn't cut very ________.
   What you need is a ________ sharpener for it.
5. Your guest has very ________ manners.
   Yes, everyone speaks ________ of him.

B. Circle the correct word in parentheses to express a negative idea.

1. I have (ever never) seen you look so tired!
   Well, I didn't get (any no) sleep last night.
2. There's (no any) ice cream left!
   I know. I didn't get (any no), either.
3. Don't you have (any no) idea where the keys are?
   Sorry, I have (any no) idea at all.
4. Haven't you (never ever) forgotten your homework?
   Well, yes, but I (ever never) said the dog ate it!
5. Didn't the tuba (ever never) get fixed?
   I don't have (no any) idea what happened to it.

Adverbs

Name____

75. Reviewing Adverbs

A. **Underline the adverb in each sentence. Above the adverb write T if it is an adverb of time, P if of place, or M if of manner.**

1. In 1865 George Washington Carver was born in Diamond Grove, Missouri, and lived on a farm there.
2. Born into slavery, he was kidnapped as a baby and taken away, from Missouri to Arkansas.
3. Carver later returned to his place of birth.
4. He went to college in Iowa, where he did very well.
5. Carver studied very hard and received a Master of Science degree in 1896.
6. He was hired by the Iowa State College of Agriculture and Mechanic Arts and worked there for the botany department.
7. Carver worked intensively to find new ways to use farm products.
8. His research was extremely useful.
9. He successfully developed hundreds of new products from peanuts, sweet potatoes, and pecans.
10. He eventually developed a substitute for rubber.

B. **Underline the correct form of the adverb in parentheses.**

1. George Washington Carver moved to Alabama and worked even (hard harder) than he had before.
2. He (more skillfully skillfully) developed more than 500 dyes and stains from almost 30 different plants.
3. Even (more amazingly amazingly), he created substitutes for products as different as bleach, cheese, ink, sugar, and shoe polish!
4. Appreciation for Carver's valuable work grew (more steadily steadily).
5. President Franklin D. Roosevelt (rightfully more rightfully) chose to honor Carver with a national monument dedicated to him in 1943.

Name____

C. Complete each sentence with the correct word in parentheses.

(good, well) 1. George Washington Carver is a ________ example of achieving success through hard work.

(ever, never) 2. We should ________ forget to work hard and do our best.

(any, no) 3. Carver's story shows us that ________ challenge is too great.

(good, well) 4. His example serves us ________.

(any, no) 5. If you truly do your best, ________ circumstance can stand in your way.

George Washington Carver worked hard to overcome obstacles and find success. Give an example of how you can work hard to find success.

Try It Yourself

Write three sentences about a race you have watched or been in. Use adverbs of time, place, and manner. Use an adverb in a comparison.

____

____

____

Check Your Own Work

Choose a piece of writing from your portfolio, a work in progress, an assignment from another class, or a letter. Revise it, using the skills you have reviewed. The checklist will help you.

✔ Have you chosen your adverbs of time, place, and manner carefully?

✔ Have you used the correct form of the adverb in comparisons?

✔ Have you used only one negative word in a sentence to express a negative idea?

Name ______________________________

76. Using Periods After Sentences and Abbreviations

A **period** marks the end of declarative and imperative sentences. Use a period after many abbreviations also.

DECLARATIVE *The Crane Maiden* **is one of my favorite stories.**
IMPERATIVE **Read it to me, please.**

A. Write **D** on the line if a sentence is declarative or **I** if it is imperative.

_____ 1. The poor man whispered as he released the trapped crane.

_____ 2. Spread your wings and fly away.

_____ 3. Later a young maiden asked the man and his wife for shelter.

_____ 4. Tsuru-san wished to repay the old couple's kindness.

_____ 5. I will weave a cloth for the two of you on this loom.

_____ 6. The maiden made only one request.

_____ 7. Do not watch me weave.

_____ 8. The curious old woman peeked through a crack in the door.

_____ 9. Find out what she saw.

_____ 10. Read *The Crane Maiden* by Miyoko Matsutani.

B. Write on the line the abbreviation for each word.

1. February __________
2. United States __________
3. West __________
4. Saturday __________
5. Road __________

Name ______________________________

77. Understanding State Abbreviations

A period is not used after postal abbreviations for states. Use only two capital letters for each state.

A. **Match the postal abbreviation in the first column with the correct state or district in the second column.**

_____ 1. DC a. Mississippi

_____ 2. WI b. Rhode Island

_____ 3. ID c. Wisconsin

_____ 4. KS d. Pennsylvania

_____ 5. SC e. New York

_____ 6. MS f. District of Columbia

_____ 7. PA g. Utah

_____ 8. UT h. South Carolina

_____ 9. RI i. Idaho

_____ 10. NY j. Kansas

KANSAS

B. **Write the correct postal abbreviation for each state.**

1. Arizona _____
2. California _____
3. Illinois _____
4. Michigan _____
5. Tennessee _____
6. Arkansas _____
7. Georgia _____
8. Maine _____
9. Oklahoma _____
10. Texas _____

Name____

78. Using Periods After Abbreviations and Initials

A period is used after abbreviations and initials.

TITLE **Dr. Collins**
INITIALS **M. J. Maples**

A. Add periods where needed in these sentences.

1. Today everyone knows who J K Rowling is.
2. She is the author of the best-selling Harry Potter books and has invented wonderful characters such as Harry, Ron, Hermione, and Prof Dumbledore.
3. After her books became hits in the U K market, she traveled to America.
4. In the U S market her Harry Potter books were even bigger successes.
5. Warner Bros bought the rights to make *Harry Potter and the Sorcerer's Stone* into a major movie.

B. Write on the line the correct abbreviation for the *italicized* words (excluding book titles). Use periods when necessary.

_____ 1. An author whom you may not know about is *Clive Staples* Lewis.

_____ 2. My friend, *Mary Kay,* read his book *The Lion, the Witch and the Wardrobe.*

_____ 3. My teacher, *Professor* Tweedy, said this book was part of a bigger series called the Chronicles of Narnia.

_____ 4. *Mister* Ruiz, the librarian, says seven books make up the Chronicles.

_____ 5. The *Parent Teacher Association* donated other fantasy books to the library.

Name____

79. Using Commas in Direct Address

Commas set off words in direct address from the rest of the sentence.

DIRECT ADDRESS **Karen, are you going to be a camp counselor again this summer?**

DIRECT ADDRESS **I don't know, Mark.**

A. **Add a comma or commas to set off the word in direct address in each sentence.**

1. Mark what about you?
2. Are you kidding Karen? Being a camp counselor is hard.
3. Mike turn off your alarm and get up!
4. Time to hit the showers boys.
5. Campers remember to form a line to go to breakfast.
6. Don't grab all the doughnuts Chris.
7. Stop crowding the little guys Howard.
8. Stevie what on earth are you doing to your food?
9. Line up boys for today's hike.
10. Larry don't pack all that stuff; you won't be able to carry it.
11. OK kids what shall we sing as we hike along the trail?
12. Lenny it's not a good idea to drink all your water at once.
13. Where are your hiking boots DeShawn?
14. David do you have the compass?
15. Let's stop and have lunch campers!

B. **Complete each sentence with a person's name in direct address. Use commas where necessary.**

(a classmate's name) 1. __________ please lend me a pencil.

(a friend's name) 2. Let's meet after school to play __________.

(a family member's name) 3. __________ may I come with you?

(your teacher's name) 4. __________ could you repeat that, please?

(a team member's name) 5. Throw me the ball __________!

Name____

80. Using Commas After Yes and No

A comma is used after the word *yes* or *no* when it introduces a sentence.

Ann:	**Do you want to play a game?**
Bill:	**Yes, let's play a guessing game!**
Ann:	**Let's see. I'm thinking of something in this classroom.**
Bill:	**Is it large?**
Ann:	**No, it isn't large.**

Add a comma where needed in each sentence.

1. No it isn't tiny.
2. Yes it fits in a desk drawer.
3. No it isn't heavy.
4. No it isn't soft.
5. No it isn't expensive.
6. Yes every student has one.
7. No it doesn't have a sharp point.
8. No it isn't round.
9. Yes it can be made of wood.
10. No it isn't square.
11. Yes it can be made of plastic too.
12. Yes it has lines on it.
13. Yes it has numbers on it.
14. Yes you can measure with it.
15. What is the object? ______________

Name____

81. Using Commas Separating Words in a Series

A comma is used to separate words in a series.

Maria, Sonia, and Kim were invited to our picnic at the beach.

A. Add a comma where needed in each group of sentences.

1. We bought picnic food at the store.
   We bought ham bread and cheese.
   We also bought chips fruit and drinks.
2. My mother wasn't very optimistic.
   She brought insect repellent wound disinfectant and sun screen.
   She also brought a flashlight a radio and extra gas for the car.
3. My friends and I just wanted to have fun!
   We had swim masks fins and snorkel tubes.
   We had towels pillows and umbrellas.
4. Walking along the beach was fun.
   We saw sailboats water skis and pedal craft.
   We collected shells smooth glass and driftwood.
5. Before going home, we visited the souvenir shop.
   We got postcards key chains and straw hats.
   We bought film T-shirts and snacks.

B. Complete each sentence with words in a series. Add commas where needed.

(add nouns) 1. We brought __________ __________ and __________ for Kim's birthday.

(add verbs) 2. We __________ __________ and __________ at our friend's party.

(add adjectives) 3. We were __________ __________ and __________ after finishing all the food and games.

(add nouns) 4. Kim's favorite presents were the __________ __________ and __________.

(add nouns) 5. I hope I get __________ __________ and __________ for my birthday!

Punctuation & Capitalization

Name____

82. Using Commas with Direct Quotations

A comma is often used to set off a **direct quotation**—the exact words of a speaker.

SPEAKER'S EXACT WORDS **"I have a good joke to tell," said Pat.**

SPEAKER'S EXACT WORDS **"Let's hear it," said Jim.**

Add commas where needed in each sentence.

1. "I'll bet you haven't heard this one" said Pat.
2. "We'll see" replied Jim.
3. "An elephant goes into an ice cream shop" began Pat.
4. "I want a chocolate sundae with all the trimmings" said the elephant to the counter attendant.
5. "I'm sorry" said the surprised attendant. "We don't serve elephants."
6. "Oh, come on, it's a hot day, and I really want a sundae" said the elephant.
7. "I'll have to ask my boss" said the attendant.
8. "Go right ahead, and tell her I want a super-sized sundae" replied the hot and hungry elephant.
9. "Sir, uh, my boss says it's OK to serve you" announced the attendant.
10. "That's great; make that sundae for me now" said the elephant.
11. "Here you are, a super-sized sundae, for only $50.00" said the attendant.
12. "You've got to be kidding" said the shocked elephant.
13. "Hey, you're lucky you have it" said the attendant.
14. "You know, we have never served an elephant in here before" he added.
15. "At these high prices, I'm not surprised" said the elephant.

Name____

83. Reviewing Commas

Add commas where needed in each sentence.

1. "Today was the worst day of my life" said Joey.
2. "What happened Joey?" asked Miriam.
3. "Well, you know I deliver the morning newspaper" replied Joey.
4. "Yes I know" said Miriam.
5. "Here's what happened. It was with the Murphy's dog" said Joey.
6. "You mean the black white and brown one that lives down the block?" asked Miriam.
7. "Yes that's the one" said Joey.
8. "Tell me what happened Joey"said Miriam.
9. "It's embarrassing Miriam" said Joey.
10. "Joey it can't be all that bad!" exclaimed Miriam.
11. "That dog jumped up licked my face and then tore my shirt" said Joey.
12. "That's terrible" said Miriam.
13. "No matter what I did, he wouldn't stop" said Joey.
14. "You called for help Joey?" asked Miriam.
15. "Yes I did" replied Joey.
16. "I'm sure Ms. Murphy come out of her house when she heard you" said Miriam.
17. "Yes and then she started yelling at me and saying I was scaring her dog!" exclaimed Joey.
18. "Oh, how strange" said Miriam. "What did you do then?"
19. "I threw a newspaper at the dog jumped on my bike and got away as fast as I could" said Joey.
20. "You're right. That is embarrassing" said Miriam.

Name____

84. Recognizing Apostrophes Showing Ownership

The **apostrophe** is used to show ownership or possession. To show that one person owns something, place an apostrophe and -*s* ('s) after the singular noun. To show that more than one person owns something, place an apostrophe after the *s* that indicates the noun is plural. If a plural noun does not end in *s*, place an apostrophe and -*s* ('s) after the noun.

ONE OWNER	**Joey's bicycle**
MORE THAN ONE OWNER	**the Murphys' dog**
PLURAL WORD NOT ENDING IN *S*	**the children's newspaper routes**

A. Write the singular possessive of each noun.

1. Miriam ____________________ friend
2. animal ____________________ behavior
3. Ms. Murphy ____________________ reaction
4. Joey ____________________ escape
5. newspaper boy ____________________ story
6. the boy ____________________ mother
7. the woman ____________________ apology
8. dog ____________________ new chain
9. Max ____________________ new route
10. the family ____________________ peace of mind

B. Write the plural possessive of each noun in the list.

1. actresses	______________	6. ladies	______________
2. bugs	______________	7. men	______________
3. cousins	______________	8. politicians	______________
4. grandchildren	______________	9. sheep	______________
5. horses	______________	10. teachers	______________

Name____

85. Recognizing Apostrophes in Contractions

An apostrophe marks the place where one or more letters have been left out in a contraction.

COMPLETE FORM	**I am**	**madam**	**let us**
CONTRACTED FORM	**I'm**	**ma'am**	**let's**

A. Write a contraction in place of the *italicized* word or words in each sentence.

__________ 1. *It is* too hot to stay here for our summer vacation.

__________ 2. I know! *Let us* go up north, to Canada.

__________ 3. *What is* the temperature like there?

__________ 4. *I am* not sure, but the temperature will be cooler than it is here.

__________ 5. That *does not* matter.

__________ 6. *It will* be too late to get tickets now anyway.

__________ 7. *Do not* give up so easily!

__________ 8. The *Web is* a great place to find airline tickets.

__________ 9. We *cannot* search the Web!

__________10. You mean the *computer is* down again?

B. Complete each sentence with a logical contraction.

1. __________ you have any other ideas for our vacation?
2. Well, I have one idea that __________ cost us much money.
3. __________ that?
4. __________ just turn on the hose in the backyard and run through the water!
5. I hope __________ kidding!

Punctuation & Capitalization

Name____

86. Using Exclamation Points and Question Marks

An **exclamation point** (!) is used at the end of an exclamatory sentence.
A **question mark** (?) is used at the end of an interrogative sentence.

EXCLAMATION POINT	**Watch out!**
QUESTION MARK	**What's wrong?**

A. Place an exclamation point or a question mark at the end of each sentence.

1. What did you say your last name was
   For the fifth time, it's Kubicki
2. You have a terrible memory
   I know, but what can I do
3. Did you know there are memory exercises
   You're kidding
4. No, really. And you above all people should try them
   I don't know. Do they really work

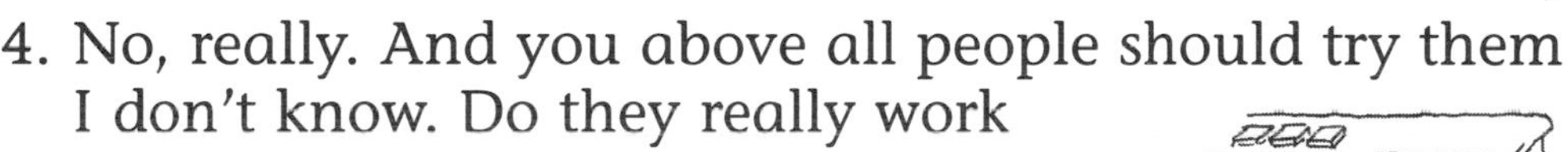

5. Come on, just try them and see
   Okay, where can I find them

B. Write three exclamatory sentences and two interrogative sentences. Use exclamation points and question marks.

1. ____

   ____
2. ____

   ____
3. ____

   ____
4. ____

   ____
5. ____

   ____

Name________________________________

87. Using Quotation Marks

Quotation marks are used before and after the exact words of a speaker—a direct quotation.

Many people have made historic statements.

DIRECT QUOTATION **"Give me liberty or give me death!" (Patrick Henry)**

A. Add quotation marks where needed in each sentence.

"OPEN SESAME"

1. May I help you? asked the librarian.
2. Yes, please, I said.
3. I'm looking for a dictionary of famous quotations, I added.
4. Perhaps you will enjoy looking at a dictionary of quotations, she said.
5. Thank you so much for your help, I said.

B. Add quotation marks where needed in each sentence.

1. P. T. Barnum of the famous circus said, There's a sucker born every minute.
2. The only way to have a friend is to be one, noted Ralph Waldo Emerson.
3. Shakespeare, in *Hamlet*, said, Neither a borrower nor a lender be.
4. To infinity and beyond! cried Buzz Lightyear in *Toy Story*.
5. God bless us every one, said Tiny Tim in Charles Dickens's *A Christmas Carol*.
6. Open, Sesame! are famous words from the *Arabian Nights*.
7. I came, I saw, I conquered, Julius Caesar has been quoted as saying.
8. President Harry Truman said, If you can't stand the heat, get out of the kitchen.
9. Who first said, Absence makes the heart grow fonder?
10. President John F. Kennedy said, Ask not what your country can do for you; ask what you can do for your country.

Name____

88. Using Capital Letters

The first word in every sentence begins with a **capital letter**. A proper noun begins with a capital letter. The names of months, days of the week, and holidays begin with capital letters.

My cousin Sarah was born in September.

Use the proofreading symbol (≡) to show which letters should be capitalized.

1. benjamin franklin was one of america's Founding Fathers.
2. he was born in boston, massachusetts, in 1706.
3. he became a printer, learning from his brother james.
4. franklin moved to philadelphia.
5. in philadelphia franklin published *Poor Richard: An Almanac.*
6. he married and had three children: william, francis, and sarah.
7. he experimented with electricity and wrote the book *Experiments and Observations on Electricity.*
8. this book was published in london.
9. franklin traveled in europe, visiting england and france.
10. Later he became a member of the continental congress.
11. in 1776 he signed the declaration of independence.
12. the declaration of independence was an important part of united states history.
13. franklin also helped negotiate treaties between america and great britain and france.
14. late in his life he acted as president of the pennsylvania society for promoting the abolition of slavery.
15. franklin died in philadelphia in 1790.

Benjamin Franklin gave his time to doing research and to helping his country develop. Give an example of a worthwhile activity that you can give your time to.

Name____

89. Working with Capital Letters

> The first word in a direct quotation always begins with a capital letter.
>
> **"Let's talk about test-taking strategies," said the teacher.**
> **The class replied, "Good idea!"**

A. **Use the proofreading symbol (≡) to show which letters should be capitalized. Add quotation marks where needed.**

1. what should you do first? asked the teacher.
2. Joe said, write your name on your test paper!
3. yes, and then what? continued the teacher.
4. can you tell us? asked Silvia.
5. be sure to look over all of the test before you start, said the teacher.
6. check on the back of the page for questions, added Billy.
7. Maria asked, then what?
8. start with something you know you can do well, said the teacher.
9. She added, save your biggest block of time for the hardest part.
10. finish with something you can do quickly, the teacher continued.

B. **Answer the questions below with true sentences. Write direct quotations, using punctuation and capital letters where needed.**

1. What is one thing your teacher said to you today?

   ____

2. What is one thing your best friend said to you?

   ____

3. What is one thing a classmate said to you?

   ____

4. What is one thing a family member said to you?

   ____

5. What is one thing someone said on TV yesterday or today?

   ____

Name____

90. Working with Capital Letters

An abbreviation begins with a capital letter if the word itself begins with a capital letter when it is written in full. An initial and the pronoun *I* are written as capital letters.
The important words in titles of books and poems begin with capital letters.

ABBREVIATION	**U.S.A.**
INITIALS	**J. K. Rowling**
PRONOUN *I*	**Tom and I are on the same team.**
BOOK TITLE	***The Blue Cat of Castle Town***
POEM TITLE	**"Shadow Dance"**

A. Use the proofreading symbol (≡) to show which letters should be capitalized.

1. guess what i am going to do this summer?
2. i am going to a computer camp.
3. it's near washington, d. c.
4. the camp is called tech smart.
5. i sent my application to p.o. box 138, alexandria, va 22314.
6. my father paid with a check from central bank.
7. now i am planning what i will take to the camp.
8. my best friend, chuck whitley, is going to go too.
9. we want to ask mr. thompson, the camp director, if we can share a room.
10. we will leave for camp on june 5.

B. Rewrite the title of each book or poem. Use capital letters where needed.

1. *computer camps in the u.s.a* ______________________
2. *basic computing for kids* ______________________
3. *how to make friends at camp* ______________________
4. "is nerd a word?" ______________________
5. "a computer mouse in the house" ______________________

Name____________________

91. Reviewing Capital Letters

A. Use the proofreading symbol (≡) to indicate which letters should be capitalized.

1. the mississippi river is the chief river of the north american continent.
2. its main course is more than 2,300 miles long.
3. it divides the u.s. mainland from north to south.
4. this great river flows from minnesota, past tennessee, down to louisiana.
5. the river ends at the gulf of mexico.
6. my favorite book about the river is *hero of the mississippi.*
7. mississippi is also the name of a southern state.
8. is mississippi an american indian word?
9. have you ever sailed down a river?
10. i would like to see the ohio and missouri rivers too.

B. Circle the group of words that is capitalized correctly.

1.	*Sailing The Mighty Mississippi*	*Sailing the Mighty Mississippi*
2.	TN means Tennessee.	Tn means Tennessee.
3.	*the World's Great Rivers*	*The World's Great Rivers*
4.	"Across the wide Missouri"	"Across the Wide Missouri"
5.	*Safety for Swimmers*	*Safety For Swimmers*
6.	"My boat won't float"	"My Boat Won't Float"
7.	mississippi chamber of commerce	Mississippi Chamber of Commerce
8.	New Orleans, Louisiana	New orleans, Louisiana
9.	Sail on the Memphis Belle!	Sail on the memphis belle!
10.	Captain heath and crew	Captain Heath and crew

Name____

92. Reviewing Punctuation and Capitalization

A. Add periods where needed in each sentence.

1. I like to watch videos and read on weekends
2. I like reading too
3. One book I really like is called *The ABC Zoo*
4. Buy it at that new bookstore
5. It's at Brookfield Ave and 13th St , on the corner

B. Write the abbreviations for the following words. Add periods if needed.

1. Thursday __________
2. September __________
3. North __________
4. Post Office __________
5. your state __________

C. Add commas and apostrophes where needed in each sentence.

1. Yes the reptile house is my favorite part of the zoo.
2. I like seeing the turtles lizards and snakes.
3. Did you know that a turtles mouth has no teeth?
4. Turtles eat flies lettuce and leaves.
5. Did you know that some lizards tails can grow back if they get cut off?
6. Lizards arent plant eaters; they prefer insects.
7. Snakes can live in the water in trees or on land.
8. No snakes dont feel wet when you touch them.
9. Snakes eat insects eggs rodents and small mammals.
10. I cant wait to visit the zoo again!

Punctuation & Capitalization

CONTINUED

Name____

D. Add quotation marks, exclamation points, and question marks.

1. Who was that mysterious girl
2. She said, I am Princess Charlotte of Windsor Castle.
3. What strange clothes she wore
4. I must be dreaming, said Terrie.
5. Was she really a princess

E. Use the proofreading symbol (≡) to indicate which letters should be capitalized in each sentence.

1. terrie and her parents were spending the summer in chiswick, england.
2. each day mrs. wright took terrie to kew botanic gardens.
3. terrie met princess charlotte in what was called the bamboo garden.
4. what strange thing did terrie discover at the kew museum?
5. you can find out if you read the *mysterious girl in the garden.*

Try It Yourself

Write three sentences about a trip you have been on. Punctuate correctly. Capitalize proper nouns. Put direct quotations in quotation marks.

____

____

____

Check Your Own Work

Choose a piece of writing from your portfolio, a work in progress, an assignment from another class, or a letter. Revise it, using the skills you have reviewed. The checklist will help you.

✔ Have you ended your sentences with the correct mark of punctuation?

✔ Have you followed the rules for commas?

✔ Have you used quotation marks before and after the exact words of the speaker?

✔ Have you capitalized all proper nouns?

Name ______________________________

93. Understanding Synonyms

Synonyms are words that have the same or almost the same meanings. Although some synonyms have exactly the same meanings, many synonyms have slightly different meanings. Use the dictionary to help you choose the best synonyms.

SYNONYMS **Pioneers crossed the prairies in their wagons.**
Pioneers crossed the plains in their wagons.

Write on the line a synonym for the word in parentheses.

1. The pioneer girl (wished)______________ to be back in the East with her cousins.
2. Her family now lived in a log (house) ______________ in the north woods of Wisconsin.
3. Her father (constructed) ______________ this home.
4. This (home) ______________ was sturdy and strong.
5. One of her (jobs) ______________ was to weed the garden.
6. She also helped her mother (clean) ______________ the clothes.
7. This was (hard) ______________ work that took all day.
8. Life was not easy for these (settlers) ______________.
9. Sometimes she felt sad and (friendless) ______________.
10. When she felt lonely, she wrote all of her thoughts in her (journal) ______________.
11. She climbed the (large) ______________ tree next to the river for fun.
12. She wished she had a (buddy) ______________ nearby to play with.
13. It was very dark in the (woods) ______________ at night.
14. Sometimes she felt (scared) ______________ at night when a wolf howled.
15. Her (dad) ______________ protected the family from any harm.

Name____

94. Working with Synonyms

Complete each sentence with a synonym for the *italicized* word.

people	**believed**	**well known**	**town**	**worked**
mother	**wrote**	**disturbed**	**wanted**	**received**

1. Rachel Carson was a writer, scientist, and ecologist born and raised in the *village* __________ of Springdale, Pennsylvania.
2. From her *mom* __________ she learned to love nature.
3. She studied marine biology and also *got* __________ a master's degree in zoology.
4. She *labored* __________ for the U.S. Bureau of Fisheries as a writer and scientist.
5. She *composed* __________ about conservation and natural resources.
6. Her study of the ocean, *The Sea Around Us*, became *famous* __________.
7. She *desired* __________ to teach people to love and find wonder in nature.
8. She *thought* __________ human beings were an important part of the natural world but a part that had the power to hurt it.
9. It *troubled* __________ her that pesticides were being misused.
10. She wrote *Silent Spring*, which asked *humans* __________ to look differently at the natural world, with a view to protecting it.

Rachel Carson cared deeply for the natural world and all its creatures. Give an example of a caring thing you can do for the natural world.

Word Study Skills

Name____

95. Understanding Antonyms

Antonyms are words that have opposite meanings.

ANTONYMS **Summer camp can be a boring or an interesting experience.**
People who are outgoing enjoy camp more than shy people do.

A. Write on the line an antonym for the *italicized* word in each sentence.

cautious **followers** **glum** **lenient** **tasty**

1. In camp activities some people are *leaders*, and some are ______________.
2. Some campers are *adventurous*, while others are ______________.
3. Some camp counselors are *strict*, and others are ______________.
4. Some people find camp food *bland*; others find it ______________.
5. First days at camp find people either *cheerful* or ______________.

B. Write on the line an antonym for the *italicized* word(s) in each sentence that makes the sentence true.

surplus **sturdy** **extinguish** **Help** **important**

__________ 1. A camping tent should be made of *flimsy* material.
__________ 2. Having a good first-aid kit is *unimportant*.
__________ 3. A *shortage* of safe drinking water is necessary.
__________ 4. Always *build up* a fire before leaving the site.
__________ 5. *Hurt* the environment by picking up litter at campsites.

C. Draw a line from each word in the first column to its antonym in the second column.

exhausted	clear
flawed	unhappy
hazy	rested
content	fresh
stale	perfect

Name____________________

96. Working with Antonyms

Circle an antonym for the *italicized* word in each sentence.

ANIMALS

1. Chameleons *keep* their color for protection.
   (change maintain conceal)
2. A burrow is a *dangerous* place for a fox to spend the winter.
   (rich wet secure)
3. Monkeys *conceal* their teeth when they are angry.
   (grind use show)
4. Bear cubs are cute but they may be more *timid* than you think.
   (aggressive awkward tame)
5. A newborn meadow mouse is as *heavy* as a feather.
   (large light smelly)

SCHOOL DAYS

6. Before the hockey game the visiting team *packed* their equipment.
   (cleaned opened unloaded)
7. There was a *narrow* central aisle in the new auditorium.
   (clear wide curving)
8. None of the students could do the *simple* equation in five minutes.
   (plain complete complicated)
9. An *unimportant* message was sent to the principal.
   (urgent useless unnecessary)
10. The *dull* student could not be easily confused.
    (perplexed uninterested bright)

Name____

97. Identifying Homophones

Homophones are words that sound alike, may be spelled differently, and have different meanings.

HOMOPHONES		
	bear	**(a large, furry mammal with a short tail)**
	bare	**(not covered or clothed)**
	meat	**(edible protein food from animals)**
	meet	**(to be introduced to, to come upon a person)**

Circle the correct homophone in parentheses.

ICEBERGS

1. An iceberg is a giant floating (piece peace) of ice from a glacier.
2. When ship captains (sea see) an iceberg, they steer around it.
3. At night it can be hard to detect exactly (where wear) an iceberg is.
4. The *Titanic* hit an iceberg in the dark of (knight night).
5. Many of the *Titanic*'s passengers (died dyed) in that terrible accident.

AGRICULTURE

6. Scientists are always searching (for four) better ways to grow food.
7. One (weigh way) they try to do this is through gene manipulation.
8. They may make changes in the structure of plant (sells cells).
9. They may take DNA from one animal and place it (inn in) another animal.
10. (Through Threw) genetics, scientists have made many vegetables bigger and more resistant to disease.

DEFINITIONS

11. The jackrabbit is a (hair hare), not a true rabbit.
12. A (not knot) is the unit of speed used by ships and airplanes.
13. (Dew Do) is moisture from the atmosphere that condenses in drops on cool surfaces at night.
14. The long hair that grows on the neck of a horse is called the (main mane).
15. A (maul mall) is where there are many stores and shops.

Name____

98. Using To, Too, and Two

To, too, and *two* are easily confused, because they sound alike. These words are homophones. *To* means "in the direction of a person, place, or thing." *Too* means "also, more than enough." *Two* means "the number 2."

To **He returned the book about bees to the school library.**
Too **He returned other library books too.**
Two **He usually reads about two library books a week.**

Complete each sentence with *to, too,* or *two.*

1. The _____ main groups of bees are social bees and solitary bees.
2. Sometimes _____ bees must carry all the nectar.
3. A beeline is the shortest route back _____ the hive.
4. _____ or more worker bees stand guard at the hive entrance.
5. A bee carries nectar _____ the hive in its honey stomach.
6. When a colony becomes _____ crowded, the old queen stops laying eggs.
7. The old queen and some workers swarm _____ a new location.
8. A young queen bee can lay eggs _____ days after mating.
9. Settlers sometimes took honeybees with them _____ the West.
10. In that way, settlers had access _____ a fresh supply of honey and beeswax.
11. Bees can sting one another _____ death.
12. Some people can die from bee stings _____.
13. Twenty-_____ bee muscles are used for stinging.
14. Wasps and yellow jackets sting _____.
15. Some animals, such as honey badgers, are not affected by bee stings as they try to get _____ honeycombs in the hives.

Word Study Skills

Name____

99. Using Their, There, and They're

Their, there, and *they're* are easily confused because they sound alike. These words are homophones. *Their* is an adjective. It shows ownership or possession. *There* is an adverb. It shows place. *They're* is a contraction. It means "they are."

THEY'RE **My neighbors are so lucky; they're going to Brazil.**
THEIR **Their tickets are ready and their bags are packed!**
THERE **I would love to go there too.**

Complete each sentence with *their, there,* or *they're.*

1. More people live __________ than in the rest of South America.
2. __________ official language is Portuguese.
3. More bananas are grown __________ than in any other nation.
4. __________ the chief exports, along with cacao beans and cattle.
5. Much of the world's coffee is grown __________.
6. __________ are two major geographical regions—the lowlands and the highlands.
7. __________ physical characteristics are different—tropical forest in the lowlands and mountainous terrain in the highlands.
8. The mighty Amazon river is __________, although it begins in Peru.
9. __________ are more than 4,600 miles of coastline and beaches in Brazil.
10. __________ visited by tourists from all over the world.
11. The people __________ are considered some of the most attractive in the world.
12. __________ a mixture of characteristics from the Portuguese, Africans, and native Indians.
13. __________ cultural traditions vary according to the geographical regions.
14. __________ music, food, and traditional clothing can be quite different.
15. Cultural artifacts are on display in many museums __________.

Name______________________________

100. Working with Contractions

A **contraction** is formed by joining two words together.
An apostrophe takes the place of the missing letter or letters.

ONE LETTER MISSING	**I'm**	**(I am)**
	ma'am	**(madam)**
TWO LETTERS MISSING	**we'll**	**(we will)**
	they've	**(they have)**

On the line write a contraction in place of the *italicized* words in each sentence.

__________ 1. *I have* been reading about a woman named Dolores Fernandez Huerta.

__________ 2. Today *she is* an influential labor leader and a social activist.

__________ 3. Doing what most Hispanic women years ago *did not*, she went to college.

__________ 4. She became a teacher but *was not* satisfied with the job.

__________ 5. She *could not* be happy when some of her students came to school barefoot and hungry.

__________ 6. She decided *she would* work not only for children but also for farm workers and others living and working in brutal conditions.

__________ 7. Earlier *she had* met César Chávez, another activist, and together they formed the United Farm Workers union.

__________ 8. Huerta *was not* afraid to bring together very different groups to fight for the rights of migrant farm workers.

__________ 9. She *did not* hesitate to march in protests that put her in personal danger.

__________ 10. *She has* promised to use only nonviolent tactics in her social protests.

Dolores Fernandez Huerta has worked hard for social justice. Give an example of an injustice you would be willing to try to change.

Name____

101. Understanding Compound Words

Compound words are two or more words joined together to make one new word.

ONE WORD +	ONE WORD =	COMPOUND WORD	ONE WORD +	ONE WORD =	COMPOUND WORD
book	**mark**	**bookmark**	**chalk**	**board**	**chalkboard**

Circle the word in each group that is a compound word.

1. compost	earthworm	centipede
2. conditioner	shampoo	hairbrush
3. airtight	resistant	container
4. rockets	universe	spacecraft
5. tidal	marine	seashore
6. asbestos	heatproof	protection
7. lifeguard	safety	observer
8. youthful	energetic	teenage
9. reporter	newspaper	editorial
10. earphones	portable	battery
11. sailboat	yacht	kayak
12. luggage	suitcase	baggage
13. envelope	letter	mailbox
14. signature	identification	fingerprint
15. clothespin	laundry	detergent
16. umbrella	lightning	raindrop
17. stationery	paperweight	writing
18. paintbrush	easel	turpentine
19. reader	bookworm	student
20. cookie	cupcake	brownie

Name____

102. Reviewing Word Study Skills

A. On the line write a contraction in place of the *italicized* words. Write **A** above the antonyms and **S** above the synonyms in each sentence.

1. __________ *Do not* shout but whisper in a library
2. __________ *You will* finish dinner and then start your homework
3. __________ The small sweatshirt *did not* fit her tiny body.

B. Complete the paragraph with the homophones below.

to too two their there they're

The ancient Incas built Machu Picchu, for which __________ still remembered. The ruins of the city are located in the Andes Mountains, the center of __________ empire. Because the site is __________ rugged for cars and buses, __________ are only __________ ways __________ reach it, hiking on foot or riding a llama. Which way would you choose to get __________ the top of Machu Picchu?

Try It Yourself

Write three sentences about an imaginary or real place you would like to visit. Use synonyms and antonyms, contractions, and at least one set of homophones.

____

____

____

Check Your Own Work

Choose a piece of writing from your portfolio, a work in progress, an assignment from another class, or a letter. Revise it, using the skills you have reviewed. The checklist will help you.

- ✔ Have you used a dictionary or thesaurus to find synonyms and antonyms?
- ✔ Were you careful in your use and spelling of all homophones?
- ✔ Have you formed all contractions correctly?

Name ____________________

103. Writing Sentences in Order

Sentences in a paragraph should be arranged in correct order. Use words that show sequence and the order in which things happen.

First, the detective took out his magnifying glass.
Then, he carefully studied the clues before him.

A. Number each set of sentences in the correct order (1–5) to make a paragraph.

_____ Finally, you have solved the mystery.

_____ First, read about Dr. Haledjian and the cave paintings.

_____ Then question yourself about that ancient scene.

_____ To meet a famous detective, open *Two-Minute Mysteries.*

_____ Next, picture in your mind a dinosaur being chased by hunters.

_____ As you read, notice the drops of paint on the neighbor's path.

_____ Then think again about the short and long spaces between drops.

_____ Finally, you decide that he must testify.

_____ Next, read about his denials.

_____ Turn to the puzzle concerning the murder witness.

_____ Then check the shelves for *Encyclopedia Brown and the Case of the Dead Eagles.*

_____ Are you interested in more than a two-minute mystery?

_____ You will find that he is the author of the Encyclopedia Brown series.

_____ Finally, you will have found a longer puzzle to solve.

_____ If so, look for another book by Donald J. Sobol.

Name____

B. Number each set of sentences in the correct order (1–5) to make a paragraph.

_____ Next, the early Romans used bricks and stones to build arch bridges.

_____ Bridges have been made from a variety of materials.

_____ Nature provided the first building materials, such as logs and vines.

_____ Finally, iron, steel, and concrete became the most widely used materials in bridge construction.

_____ Then, during the Middle Ages, stone and wood were used to form drawbridges across moats.

_____ An electromagnet is easy to assemble.

_____ Finally, fasten a third wire from the negative pole of the battery to the "on" part of the switch.

_____ Next, attach one wire from the nail to the positive pole on a dry-cell battery.

_____ Then connect the second wire on the nail to the "off" part of a switch.

_____ First, wrap two long wires around a piece of metal, such as a nail.

_____ After the blending, pour the pulp mixture onto a screen, so that the water separates from the pulp.

_____ Last, remove the book and turn the screen upside down to let the flattened paper pulp dry.

_____ To make your own paper, put torn-up newspaper in a container and cover it with water.

_____ Put a sheet of wax paper and a heavy book over the pulp on the screen.

_____ Next, put the wet paper into a blender with more water and blend.

Name ___

104. Finding the Exact Word

Use exact words to add color, interest, and excitement to a paragraph. Nouns, verbs, adjectives, and adverbs can be colorful and descriptive.

GENERAL **People participate in politics because of their beliefs.**
DESCRIPTIVE **People fight passionately for their political beliefs.**

Underline the word(s) in each sentence that add color, interest, or excitement. Some are nouns or adjectives, others are verbs, and others are adverbs.

1. Aung San Suu Kyi reigns as a political hero in Myanmar (the country formerly known as Burma).
2. She led a quiet life at Oxford University in England until her mother became ill.
3. Aung San Suu Kyi returned to Burma in 1988 to nurse her dying mother.
4. While she was there, she courageously spoke out in favor of democracy at political rallies.
5. A believer in nonviolence, she bravely faced soldiers with rifles.
6. The Burmese government crushed the pro-democracy movement and tortured and killed many protestors.
7. In 1990 Aung San Suu Kyi's political party easily won a majority of votes, but the existing government refused to step down.
8. She was arrested and confined to her house, unable to return to her husband and children in England.
9. Her husband, a victim of cancer, was refused permission to see his wife before he died.
10. Because of her belief in democracy and her painful personal sacrifices for the cause, Aung San Suu Kyi was given the Nobel Prize for Peace.

Aung San Suu Kyi has shown great personal and political courage. Give an example of how you can act courageously.

Name____

105. Using Similes in Writing

A **simile** compares two seemingly unlike things that actually have something in common. The words *like* and *as* are used in similes.

SIMILE WITH *LIKE* **The sun sparkled like an enormous diamond.**
SIMILE WITH *AS* **The clouds in the blue sky were as fluffy as cotton balls.**

A. Complete the simile in each sentence with *like* or *as.*

1. The soft grass was as green __________ emeralds.
2. The gentle breeze was __________ a mother's soft touch.
3. The stream stretched out in the distance __________ a long blue ribbon.
4. The new park benches were as comfortable __________ couches.
5. Birds in the trees sang as energetically __________ choirs in church.

B. Look at sentences 1–5 in Part A again. Identify the things being compared in each simile. Write them on the lines.

1. Sentence A-1: ______________ ______________
2. Sentence A-2: ______________ ______________
3. Sentence A-3: ______________ ______________
4. Sentence A-4: ______________ ______________
5. Sentence A-5: ______________ ______________

C. Complete the simile in each sentence. Use words from the list.

jewels helicopter rubies snake tiger

1. The cardinal's feathers were as red as __________.
2. The house cat tracked a bird like a __________ would its prey.
3. The flowers along the path were as colorful as __________.
4. A hummingbird hovered above a bloom like a __________ in the sky.
5. The path wound its way through the park like a __________.

Name ____

106. Expanding Sentences

Some sentences give only a simple fact. Other sentences include details that help give the reader a clear picture. Details can tell *when, where, what kind, how far,* and *how.*

FACT	**The Inca lived.**
DETAIL TELLING *WHEN*	**The Inca lived at the time of the Spanish conquest.**
DETAIL TELLING *WHERE*	**The Inca lived in what is now Peru and parts of Ecuador, Chile, Bolivia, and Argentina.**
DETAIL TELLING *WHAT KIND*	**The Inca lived in a highly organized society.**
DETAIL TELLING *HOW*	**Most of the time the Inca lived peacefully.**

A. Look at the kind of detail listed at the left of each sentence. Then underline the words in the sentence that describe that information.

where 1. The Inca's territory covered about 3,000 square miles from north to south and from the Pacific coast to the high Andes.

how 2. The Inca remained connected through a sophisticated system of roads.

what kind 3. Some of these roads stretched over the Andean gorges in the form of fiber cable suspension bridges.

how far 4. Trained relay runners delivering messages could cover around 150 miles a day, using these roads and bridges.

what kind 5. Because of this road and bridge system, the Incan army had quick access to areas where there might be trouble.

B. Expand these sentences by telling *how, where, what kind,* or *when.* Write words that make the sentences true for you.

1. ________ (how) my friend invited me ________ (where).
2. I ate breakfast ________ (how) ________ (when).
3. ________ (when) I help my ________ (what kind) friend with chores.
4. My mother ________ (how) turned off the TV ________ (where).
5. My teacher ________ (when) helps me with ________ (what kind) questions.

Revising a Paragraph

Name____________________

107. Trimming Long Sentences

Sentences that contain too many words or ideas should be trimmed or broken up to make shorter sentences.

Africa is one of the seven continents, and it has many countries in it, including Egypt, where you can see pyramids.

Africa is one of the seven continents. It has many countries in it, including Egypt, where you can see pyramids.

Break up each of these sentences into two or three shorter, clearer sentences.

1. Egypt is a desert country located in northeast Africa, and there the climate is very hot and dry all the time.

2. Most of the people in Egypt live along the Nile River in the part of the river called the delta, where the land is fertile.

3. Many Egyptian people know how to speak French or English in addition to Arabic, which is the official language of Egypt.

4. The economy of Egypt is based on agriculture, primarily the growing of cotton, wheat, corn, and rice, and some oil refining, some manufacturing, and tourism.

Name ____

5. Basketball was invented in America in December of 1891, and James Naismith thought of the idea that winter.

____

____

____

6. Most people don't know that basketball was first played with a soccer ball, and that was because the ball we use for basketball didn't exist yet.

____

____

____

7. Wooden peach baskets were used for the first basketball games, and so the baskets weren't like the ones we play basketball with today.

____

____

____

8. In the beginning of basketball history, nine people played on each team, and now only five people play on each team.

____

____

____

Name____

108. Practicing Revision

When you revise, you take a careful look at your sentences and paragraphs and try to improve them.
Think of these questions when you revise your sentences.

a. **Have I made sure my sentences are in logical order and make sense?**
b. **Have I used interesting, colorful words to paint a clear picture?**
c. **Have I used similes where possible to add exciting comparisons?**
d. **Have I used *and, so,* and *and then* too often?**
e. **Have I expanded my sentences by adding important details?**

A. In each set, the second sentence is a revision of the first. Write the letter from above that tells how the original sentence was revised.

1. Native Americans today value their old traditions, and so they want to save them and pass them down to their children, so these traditions won't disappear.

_____ Native Americans today value their old traditions. They want to pass these down to their children, so these traditions won't disappear.

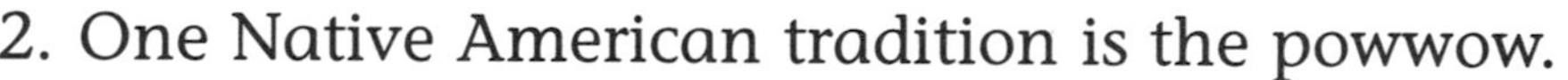

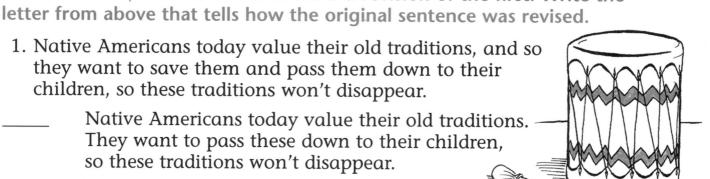

2. One Native American tradition is the powwow.

_____ One Native American tradition is the powwow, a celebration of native culture through dance and song.

3. Native Americans come to powwows in their traditional dress.

_____ Native Americans come to powwows dressed in beaded shirts and pants of softened hide, and colorful feather headdresses.

4. The rhythm of the drums encourages people to dance and sing. In the middle of the dance, men begin to beat a ceremonial drum.

_____ In the middle of the dance, men begin to beat a ceremonial drum. The rhythm of the drums encourages people to dance and sing.

5. The drums are really loud.

_____ The drums roll and boom like thunder into the night.

Name ______________________________

B. **When you see a number in parentheses before a word, look down below to the numbered directions. Follow the directions to revise the paragraph. Write the revised paragraph on the lines below.**

Finger Talk

(1) Koko the gorilla speaks with her hands. (2) Penny Patterson teaches her to talk with her fingers and shows Koko a ball and then shapes the gorilla's hands into the finger-talk word for *ball.* (3) They practice until Koko learns it. (4) This finger talk, a kind of sign language, is something of a game to Koko. (5) If you see a gorilla making interesting shapes with her fingers, it may be that Koko is talking to you.

1. In sentence 1, write a more exact word for *speaks.*
2. Trim sentence 2 to make shorter, clearer sentences. Add an order word to keep the ideas in correct order.
3. Expand sentence 3 by adding details.
4. Write sentence 4 as a simile.
5. Write another title for the paragraph.

Name____

109. Learning to Proofread

Learning to proofread will help you make your final copy perfect.

≡ **Make a capital letter.**
(SP) **Correct spelling.**
—ℓ **Omit a word or letter.**
∧ **Add a word or phrase.**
⊙ **Change end punctuation to period.**
¶ **Begin a new paragraph.**

A. Each sentence contains a mistake. Add the correct proofreading symbol to mark the places where corrections are needed.

Ferns are intresting members of the plant family.

1. Fern plants have has grown on Earth for a long time.
2. many seed-makeing plants developed from these early ferns.
3. ferns are composed of roots, stems, and leaves.
4. Ferns do not grow from seeds!
5. These plants grow spores that form in small, round clusters on underside of their leaves.
6. Wind carries these miniature spores to places where they can sprout?
7. Ferns grow in most parts of the world except in desserts.
8. More ferns grow warm climates than in cooler places.
9. some ferns look like vines climbing a tree.
10. Other ferns grow only on on rocks.

B. Use the proofreading symbols to mark the places where corrections should be made in this paragraph.

Many different forms of life are found in the ocean world? seaweed is a plant that grows in this underwater empire. Seaweed can very tiny or grow in strands exceeding 300 feet in length. At one time sailers were afraid of these emerald-colored plants, because they thought the the seaweed would encircle their ships and keep them trapped.

Name ____________________

110. The Parts of a Social Letter

A social, or friendly, letter has five parts: the **heading,** which tells the address of the writer and the date of the letter; the **greeting,** or salutation; the **body,** which is the message; the **complimentary close,** or good-bye; and the **signature,** or name of the writer. The body is the most important part of a letter.

A. Write the names of the letter parts next to the correct number.

body **complimentary close** **greeting**
heading **signature**

1. ____________________

____

2. ____________________

3. ____________________

____

____

4. ____________________

5. ____________________

B. Proofread the following parts of a social letter. Rewrite each one, adding punctuation and capital letters where needed.

1. sincerely ____________________
2. 843 lincoln highway ____________________
3. bethlehem pa 18017 ____________________
4. april 2 2003 ____________________
5. dear nicole ____________________
6. kanisha ____________________
7. your nephew ____________________
8. justin ____________________
9. july 4 2003 ____________________
10. your friend ____________________

Name____

111. The Heading of a Letter

The **heading** of a letter generally has three lines. It starts a little to the right of the center of the paper. The first word of each line begins directly under the first word of the line above it. On the first line write your street address; on the second line write your city, state, and ZIP code; and on the third line write the month, day, and year.

Each word in the heading begins with a capital letter and is written out in full, except for the state. Use the two-letter postal abbreviation for the state. A comma is placed between the name of the city and the state. Another comma is placed between the day of the month and the year.

Write each heading in correct form. Use the lines below.

1. 723 hoff street	july 19 2003	bakerton west virginia 25410
2. 8431 rio grande lane	january 29 2003	gallup new mexico 87301
3. 528 markham avenue	may 24 2003	wheatland wyoming 82201
4. 3029 glennbrook drive	august 10 2003	lansing michigan 48921
5. 95 avila street apt 2-f	october 16 2003	new york new york 10034

1. ______________________________
____
____

2. ______________________________
____
____

3. ______________________________
____
____

4. ______________________________
____
____

5. ______________________________
____
____

Letter Writing

Name ______________________________

112. The Greeting of a Letter

The greeting of the letter is the **salutation.** The greeting begins at the left-hand margin. The first word of the greeting and the person's name begin with a capital letter. A comma always follows the greeting of a social, or friendly, letter.

A. Rewrite the following greetings correctly, placing a comma after each and using capital letters where needed.

1. dear roberto ______________________
2. dear uncle mark ______________________
3. hi, amy ______________________
4. dear dr. bell ______________________
5. hello, tanya ______________________
6. dear tawanda ______________________
7. hi, paul ______________________
8. dear mr. lopez ______________________
9. hello, grandpa ______________________
10. dear mrs horowitz ______________________

B. Write the greeting for a letter to each of these persons.

1. your dentist ______________________
2. your brother ______________________
3. a cousin ______________________
4. your best friend ______________________
5. your teacher ______________________

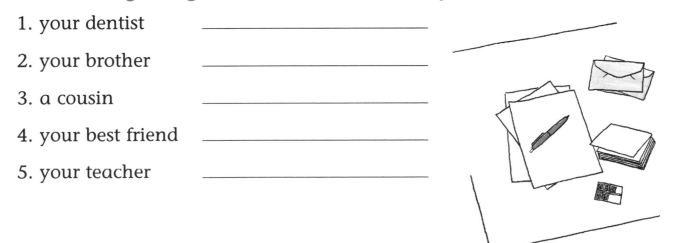

Letter Writing

Name____

113. The Complimentary Close of a Letter

In the **complimentary close** of a letter, you say good-bye. It begins on the line below the last sentence. It starts a little to the right of the center of the paper and is in line with the heading. Only the first word of the complimentary close begins with a capital letter. A comma always follows the last word of the complimentary close.

The **signature** is written directly under the first word of the complimentary close.

A. Use the proofreading symbol (≡) to show where capital letters are needed. Add the correct punctuation in each complimentary close.

1. fondly
2. your neighbor
3. with love
4. sincerely
5. your grandson
6. affectionately
7. love
8. respectfully
9. your pal
10. your classmate

B. Write a complimentary close for a letter to each of these persons.

1. a friend who has moved ______________________
2. your aunt ______________________
3. the librarian ______________________
4. a pen pal in another country ______________________
5. your coach ______________________

C. Write a greeting, complimentary close, and signature for this letter.

____

I just got home from my first day at my new school. I met a new friend, Frankie. Maybe Mr. Falbo will let us be lab partners. I hope so!

How was your first day of school? I miss the old place! Write soon and let me know how the basketball and soccer teams are doing.

____

____

Name ______________________________

114. Addressing an Envelope

An envelope should have a mailing address and a return address. In the top left corner, put your name, street address, city, state, and ZIP code. This is called the **return address.** In the middle of the envelope put the name of the person to whom you are writing, his or her street address, city, state, and ZIP code. This is called the **mailing address.**

A. Use the proofreading symbol (≡) to show which letters should be capitalized. Add punctuation marks where needed.

1. chris smith
   1811 alameda road
   Houston tx 77004

Mr james m Arnold jr
706 parkview road
junction city wi 54443

2. mr mark reed
   4135 cottage hill street apt 3-b
   claymont de 19703

dr marsha timby
4723 westbrook drive
oakville ct 06779

3. ms judith allan
   1204 duckwater road
   sparks nv 89431

ms stephanie kane
4603 livingston place
salt lake city ut 84113

Letter Writing

Name____

B. Address each envelope.

1. **Mailing address:** Ms. Marie Kamm 752 Grover Street Duluth, MN 55805

   Return address: Ms. Alma Cortes 3120 7th Avenue Birmingham, AL 35218

2. **Mailing address:** Dr. Paul Kent 32 Durham Drive Belmont, NH 03220

   Return address: Ben Singer 18 Bowler Avenue Oklahoma City, OK 73141

1.

____
____
____

____
____
____

2.

____
____
____

____
____
____

C. Find a used envelope at home or school. Is the envelope addressed correctly? On a separate piece of paper either paste or draw the envelope. Correct any mistakes.

Name ______________________________

115. E-Mails: Invitations and Acceptances

Often we receive invitations by e-mail. An invitation must include some special information. You should tell your friends the kind of event (a birthday party, a baseball game, a picnic), where they should come (the place), and when they are to come (the day, the date, and the hour).

Invitations should be answered soon after you receive them. If you are able to attend, write an e-mail of acceptance. If you are unable to attend, write an e-mail of regret.

An e-mail should have a greeting and a closing, followed by your typed name; but it does not need a heading.

A. Answer each question according to the invitation.

New Message

To...	DianaLocke@her-house.com
Cc...	
Subject:	school play

Dear Cousin Diana,

I would like to invite you to a play about Harriet Tubman that we are doing at our school. She helped people escape from slavery a long time ago, and I play her sister. The performance will be held in the auditorium of Greengrove School, 515 Fremont Park Road, Springfield, Massachusetts, on Friday, April 26, at 6:00 P.M. Maybe we can go out for pizza afterwards! I hope to see you there.

Love,
Kendra

1. Cousin Diana is invited to a ______________.

2. The play will be held at ______________.

3. It is to take place on the ______________ day of the month of ______________.

4. The performance will begin at ______________.

5. ______________ wrote the invitation to Diana.

HARRIET TUBMAN
A PLAY
GREENGROVE SCHOOL AUDITORIUM
515 FREEMONT PARK RD.
SPRINGFIELD, MA
FRIDAY, APRIL 26
6 P.M.

Letter Writing

Name____

B. Write an e-mail accepting this invitation. Mark's e-mail address is MarkSwan@xyz.com.

New Message

To...	JaimeKoga@xyz.com
Cc...	
Subject:	National Rotten Sneaker Championship

Dear Jaime,

My father is taking me to a really fun competition. It is the National Rotten Sneaker Championship to be held in Montpelier, Vermont, on March 21 at 1:30 P.M. Would you like to come with us? My dad said we will leave at 9:00 A.M. on the day of the competition, and we can pick you up on our way. I hope you will be able to come.

Your friend,
Mark

New Message

To...	
Cc...	
Subject:	

____

____

____

____

____

____

____

____

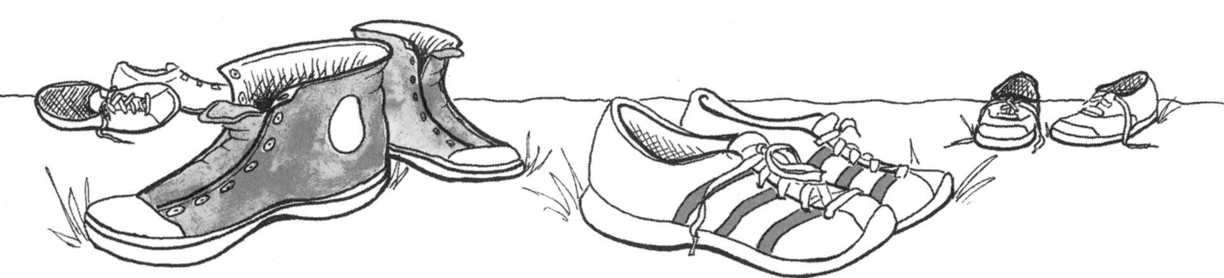

Name ______________________________

116. Proofreading Letters

A. Use the proofreading symbol (≡) to show which letters should be capitalized. Add the missing punctuation marks.

834 belgrade street
hill city sd 57745
february 24 2002

dear erik

we were sorry to hear about your skiing accident we hope that your leg heals quickly and that you will be back with us in class before long we will help you carry your books and lunch tray when you get back get well soon

your friends
the fourth grade

B. Rewrite the letter. Include all the corrections you made.

____
____
____

____

____
____
____
____
____
____

____
____

Letter Writing

Name______________________________

117. Review of a Social Letter

A. Write the following letter in correct order.

Greeting	Signature	Heading	Complimentary close
Dear Lauren	Toni	1643 Lotus Road Sioux City, IA 51101 March 27, 2002	Your friend,

Body

Our trip to Japan was so exciting! We visited several temples and tea gardens, but the place I liked best was the Kyoto School of Flower Arrangement.

The Flower Master is like a principal. It takes many years of practice before a student becomes a teacher. The Japanese have many strict rules for flower arranging. That is why it takes such a long time to learn this art.

Letter Writing

Name ______________________________

B. Rewrite the following letter, making all necessary corrections.

june 1 2002
52 midland street apt 4-C
long pond PA 18334

dear aunt felicia

the bubble machine you sent for my birthday is terrific all my friends wanted to try it when I showed them the gigantic bubbles it makes mom and pat like it too they were playing with it last night when I came home thank you for the wonderful present your gifts are always exciting surprises

your nephew
chris

____
____
____

____

____
____
____
____
____
____
____
____
____

____
____

Letter Writing

Name____

C. Address the envelope. Use the information in the heading of Chris's letter on page 131 for the return address. Add punctuation and capital letters where needed. Chris's last name is Fox also.

Mailing address: ms felicia fox 7809 mesa drive santa fe nm 87501

Letter Writing

Name ______________________________

118. Filling Out Forms

A **form** is an easy way to give information. There are forms for many different things: bicycle registrations, library cards, pet licenses, and contest entries.

- Read the entire form first.
- Answer all the questions.
- Write neatly so that the information is clear to the reader.
- Use capital letters, also called block letters, when requested.
- Write one letter or one number in each block.
- Leave one space between items if possible.
- Check over your answers.

A	N	G	E	L	A		B	O	S	C	O			
1	0		S	K	Y	L	A	R	K		L	A	N	E

A. Complete this form with your information.

Last Name First Name Middle Initial

Address

City State ZIP Code

Telephone

Male ☐ Female ☐

Date of Birth

Letter Writing

CONTINUED

Name ____

B. Fill in the correct information on the following form.

50-50 Club Raffle

Name ____

Address ____

____

Telephone ____

Seller's Name ____

C. Many companies offer rebates. Fill out this rebate form.

MANUFACTURER'S REBATE

Save $1.00 on Video Village 90-min. blank cassette tapes.

Limit one rebate per address

Send proof of purchase and rebate form to

Video Village Enterprises
Box 1620
Visual Impressions Boulevard
Jefferson City, MO 65101

- -

Name ____

Address ____

____

City State ZIP Code

Place of purchase ____

Address ____

____

City State ZIP Code

Date of purchase ____/____/____

Name ______________________________

D. Enter this contest. Give the information requested.

Bubble-Blowing Contest

Here is your chance to win paperback books of your choice—just by blowing bubbles. The contest will be held at the Albany Public Library in Albany, Oregon, on July 15 at 10:00 A.M. Each contestant will be given one jar of bubble liquid to be used in all the contest events. The three events in this contest are *First to Blow a Bubble, Biggest Bubble Blown,* and *Longest-Lasting Bubble.*

It's easy to enter.

1. You must be between the ages of 8 and 12.
2. Fill in the entry form below.
3. Entry forms must be postmarked by June 10.
4. Mail entry form to
   Children's Librarian
   Albany Public Library
   1390 Waverly Drive
   Albany, OR 97312

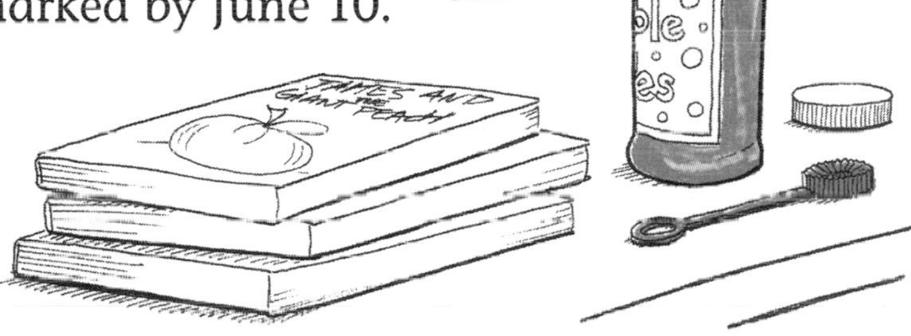

- -

ENTRY FORM

Please print.

Name ______________________________

Address ______________________________

City ______________ State__________ ZIP Code__________

Phone Number (____) ____________Date of Birth ____/____/____

Signature of Applicant ______________________________

Signature of Parent or Guardian ______________________________

CONTINUED

Name ____

E. Send a bouquet of balloons to celebrate a special occasion. Complete the form below and brighten someone's day.

Balloon Bonanza

Pleasantville, U.S.A.

Send balloons to

Name ____

Address ____

City ____________________ State ______ ZIP Code __________

Occasion ____

Date of Delivery ____

Gift sent by

Name ____

Address ____

City ____________________ State ______ ZIP Code __________

Phone Number ____

On the gift card, please write

____

____

____

____

____

____

____

Name ______________________________

119. Searching for Information on the Internet

Here are several ways to find information on the Internet.

1. If you know an Internet address that might have the information you want, type the address.

or

2. Look at the first page you see when you log onto the Internet. Does it have a section designed for students? If so, click there to start your research.

or

3. Use a search engine such as Google or Yahoo. (Yahoo has a student search engine called Yahooligans.) Type a **subject** or a **keyword** related to your research topic. The search engine will look for Web pages that match the keyword.

Try a search yourself!

- If you type in a single word, such as *dinosaurs,* the search engine will look for every site with that word. There could be thousands of sites, too many for you to look at!
- If you type two or more words, such as *big dinosaurs,* the search engine will look for every site that includes these words. Again, there may be thousands of entries for you to look at. (You don't have that much time!)
- If you type a phrase or keyword in quotation marks, such as *"big dinosaurs,"* the search engine will find all the sites that contain exactly that phrase or keyword. This still may lead you to more sites than you want to look at.
- Now try this. Type a very specific phrase, such as *big dinosaurs in Jurassic period.* Your topic is narrowed to exactly what you need information about. The list of sites will be much smaller!

Name____

A. Now answer these questions about Internet searching.

You want to find out about some wild animals that live in Africa. Look at the phrases, or keywords, below. Tell whether you think each keyword is a good one to use, a better one to use, or the best one to use by circling good, better, or best. Then tell why you think this.

1. Elephants good better best

   ____

   ____

2. Africa good better best

   ____

   ____

3. Elephants in Africa good better best

   ____

   ____

4. Wildlife preserves in Africa good better best

   ____

   ____

5. Zoos in Africa good better best

   ____

   ____

B. Circle the best phrase or keyword in each line below to use in a computer search for information.

1. planet	Mars	the red planet	solar system
2. Arctic places	treeless plain	tundra	cold ground
3. animal lover	zoologist	animal keeper	zoo person
4. yellow flowers	sunflowers	plants	flowers
5. green vegetables	food	vegetables	spinach

Name ______________________________

120. Using a Dictionary: Entries

You can learn much more than just the meanings of words when you use a **dictionary.** Here is a dictionary page. Look at the labels. Notice the many things that the **entries** tell you about the words.

Be sure to look at the **pronunciation key** at the lower right corner of the page. These symbols help you correctly pronounce the entry words.

mother ▶ mound

colored. Moths fly mostly at night. One kind of moth has larvae that eat holes in fur and wool.
moth • ***noun,*** *plural* **moths** (môthz *or* môths)

ENTRY WORD →

mother (mu*th*′ər) ***noun*** **1** a woman as she is related to her child or children; a female parent. **2** the origin, source, or cause of something [Virginia is the State known as the *mother* of Presidents.]
adjective **1** of, like, or being a mother [*mother* love; a *mother* hen]. **2** having a relationship like that of a mother [All the branches report to the *mother* company in Detroit.]
verb to care for as a mother does [We *mothered* the abandoned kittens.]
moth·er • ***noun,*** *plural* **mothers** • ***adjective*** • ***verb*** **mothered, mothering**

mother-in-law (mu*th*′ər in lô *or* mu*th*′ər in lä) ***noun*** the mother of one's wife or husband.
moth·er-in-law • ***noun,*** *plural* **mothers-in-law**

motherly (mu*th*′ər lē) ***adjective*** of or like a mother [a *motherly* hug; *motherly* concern for the orphan].
moth·er·ly • ***adjective***

mother-of-pearl (mu*th*′ər əv purl′) ***noun*** the hard, shiny layer on the inside of some seashells. Mother-of-pearl shines with different soft colors and is used in making buttons and in jewelry.
moth·er-of-pearl • ***noun***

ACCENT MARK →

motion (mō′shən) ***noun*** **1** the act or process of moving from one place to another; movement [The sea is always in *motion.*] **2** a movement of the head, arm, or other part of the body in a way that has meaning; gesture [The waiter made a beckoning *motion* to tell us that our table was ready.] **3** a formal suggestion or request made during a meeting or trial [He made a *motion* to end the meeting at 5 p.m.]
verb to move the head, hand, or other part of the body so as to show what one means or wants [The police officer *motioned* us to stop.]
mo·tion • ***noun,*** *plural for senses 2 and 3 only* **motions** • ***verb*** **motioned, motioning**

PRONUNCIATION →

motionless (mō′shən ləs) ***adjective*** not moving [He stood *motionless* at the top of the stairs.]
mo·tion·less • ***adjective***

motion picture ***noun*** *the same as* **movie.**
motion picture • ***noun,*** *plural* **motion pictures**

482

motive (mōt′iv) ***noun*** a reason that makes a person do something [What was their *motive* for inviting us to their house?]
mo·tive • ***noun,*** *plural* **motives**

motor (mōt′ər) ***noun*** a device or machine that provides the power to make something move or work [The fan has an electric *motor.*]
adjective **1** driven by a motor or engine [a *motor* bicycle]. **2** having to do with or for motors [*motor* oil; *motor* parts]. **3** of or having to do with nerves or muscles that control movement [The long illness left her with poor *motor* control.]
verb to travel by car [We *motored* through Mississippi.]
mo·tor • ***noun,*** *plural* **motors** • ***adjective*** • ***verb*** **motored, motoring**

motorboat (mōt′ər bōt) ***noun*** a boat that is run by a motor.
mo·tor·boat • ***noun,*** *plural* **motorboats**

motorcycle (mōt′ər sī kəl) ***noun*** a kind of very heavy bicycle that is run by a gasoline engine.
mo·tor·cy·cle • ***noun,*** *plural* **motorcycles**

← SYLLABLE DIVISIONS

motor vehicle ***noun*** a vehicle on wheels, having its own motor, and not running on rails or tracks. Cars, trucks, buses, and motorcycles are motor vehicles.
motor vehicle • ***noun,*** *plural* **motor vehicles**

Mott (mät), **Lucretia** (lo͞o krē′shə) 1793-1880; U.S. abolitionist and leader in the women's rights movement.
Mott, Lu·cre·ti·a

← DEFINITION

motto (mät′ō) ***noun*** **1** a brief saying that is used as a rule to live by ["Honesty is the best policy" was his *motto.*] **2** a word or phrase chosen to show the goals or ideals of a nation, club, or other organization. A motto is usually inscribed on a coin, seal, or flag ["Don't tread on me!" was the *motto* on an early U.S. flag.]
mot·to • ***noun,*** *plural* **mottoes** or **mottos**

← PART OF SPEECH

mound (mound) ***noun*** **1** a heap or hill of earth, sand, or other material [There are *mounds* of stones all over the fields.] **2** the slightly raised place from which a baseball

a	cat	ō	go	ʉ	fur	ə = a *in* ago	
ā	ape	ô	law, for	ch	chin	e *in* agent	
ä	cot, car	oo	look	sh	she	i *in* pencil	
e	ten	o͞o	tool	th	thin	o *in* atom	
ē	me	oi	oil	*th*	then	u *in* circus	
i	fit	ou	out	zh	measure		
ī	ice	u	up	ŋ	ring		

← PRONUNCIATION KEY

Research Skills

Research Skills

Name____

Use the dictionary sample on page 139 to answer these questions.

1. How many syllables do the following words have?

   motherly ________ motto ________ motionless ________

   motive ________ Mott ________ motorcycle ________

2. Who was Lucretia Mott? ____

   ____

3. When did Lucretia Mott live? ____

4. Which entry means "movie"? ____

5. What is a motive? ____

   ____

6. What is a motto usually inscribed on? ____

7. True or False: *Mother* can be a noun, an adjective, or a verb. ________

8. Which syllable should be accented, or stressed, when you say the following words?

   mother ________________ Lucretia ________________

   motionless ________________ motorcycle ________________

9. Tell whether each word is a noun, a verb, or an adjective.

   motive ________________ motionless ________________

   motto ________________ motioned ________________

10. Which word from the dictionary page would you use to complete each of the following sentences?

    My ________________ is "do the right thing."

    Mrs. Farrell made a ________________ to have the club meet weekly on Thursdays.

    The ghost seemed to be standing ________________ at the open window.

Name ______________________________

121. Using a Thesaurus

When you are writing a story, do you sometimes think that the meaning of a word is not quite right for what you want to say? A **thesaurus** can help you. It is a **reference book** that lists synonyms and antonyms for words. Synonyms are words with similar meanings, and antonyms are words with opposite meanings. A thesaurus also comes with some word-processing software programs. Look for it under "Tools."

A thesaurus can help you
- find just the right word for a sentence
- use different words, rather than the same ones over and over again

PART OF SPEECH

ENTRY WORD → **GRAY**—*N.* **gray** *or* grey, silver, dove color, pepper and salt, *chiaroscuro (It.)*; dun, drab, etc. (see *Adjectives*). ← SYNONYMS

V. **gray** *or* grey, grizzle, silver dapple.

Adj. **gray** or grey, grizzled, grizzly, griseous, ash-gray, ashen, ashy, cinereous; dingy, leaden, pearly, pearl-gray, clouded, cloudy, misty, foggy, hoary, hoar, canescent, silver, silvery, silver-gray; iron-gray, dun, drab, dappled, dapple-gray, brindle, brindled, mouse-colored, stone-colored, slate-gray; dove-grey, columbine, fulvous, taupe, oyster-white; sad, dull, somber.

gray-haired, silver-haired, gray-headed, hoary, grizzly.

See also CLOUD, DARKNESS, DULLNESS, OLDNESS, SADNESS, WHITENESS.

ANTONYMS → *Antonyms* — See CHEERFULNESS, LIGHT.

Some thesauruses are organized alphabetically. You look up the word just as you would in a dictionary. In other thesauruses, you look up the word in an index.

CONTINUED

Research Skills

Name____

1. What parts of speech may the word *gray* be?

____

2. What other words could you look up to find more synonyms and antonyms for *gray?*

____

Read these sentences. Select a synonym from the thesaurus entry on page 141 to find another word for *gray* for each sentence. Use a different synonym in each sentence.

3. The *gray-haired* miner looked as if he had been in the mine for a long time. ____________________

4. It was a *gray* morning along the rugged coast of Maine.

____

5. The *gray* house looked as if it needed a great deal of work done on it.

____

What antonym might you use in place of *gray* in this sentence?

6. The *gray-faced* man waited for the doctor. ____________________

Choose a word from the thesaurus entry on page 141 to make each sentence below interesting.

7. My grandmother's hair is ____________________.

8. When Elizabeth fainted, her face turned ____________________.

Circle the word that you think makes each sentence the most interesting.

9. We found mostly ____________________ days along the Oregon coast.

   drab　　dull　　sad

10. The ____________________ horse raced around the track in record time.

   gray　　dapple-gray　　gray-headed

Sentence Diagrams

A diagram is a picture that shows how the parts of a sentence are related. The most important parts of a sentence are the nouns and verbs.

- The simple subject of a sentence is a noun.
- The simple predicate of a sentence is a verb.

Diagramming a Simple Sentence

A. Diagramming the simple subject, simple predicate, and direct object.

1. A simple sentence has one complete thought. This simple sentence has one subject noun, one verb, and one direct object noun.

   John plays soccer.

Here's how to diagram it.

2. The main line of a diagram is a horizontal line.

   ____

3. The verb in the sentence is *plays.* Write *plays* on the center of the diagram line.

   ____________plays____________

4. Who plays? John plays. *John* is the subject. Write *John* on the line in front of plays. Draw a vertical line to separate *John* and *plays.* The vertical line should cut through the horizontal line.

   ____________John | plays____________

5. Whom or what does John play? John plays soccer. *Soccer* is the direct object. Write *soccer* on the line after *plays*. Draw a vertical line to separate *plays* and *soccer*. This vertical line should touch the horizontal line but not cut through it.

John | plays | soccer

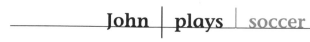

6. When the subject is a pronoun, the sentence is diagrammed in the same way as when the subject is a noun.

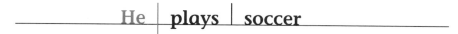

He | plays | soccer

B. Diagramming modifiers

1. A possessive form of a noun goes on a slanted line attached to the horizontal line under the noun it modifies.

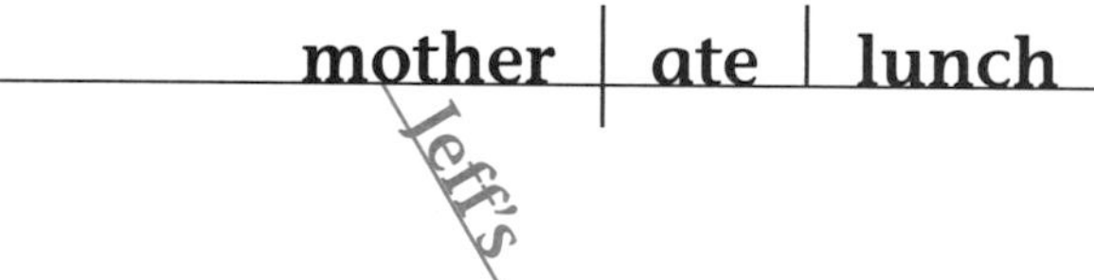

2. An adverb goes on a slanted line attached to the horizontal line under the word it modifies.

3. An adjective goes on a slanted line under the noun it modifies. If there is more than one adjective, use more than one slanted line.

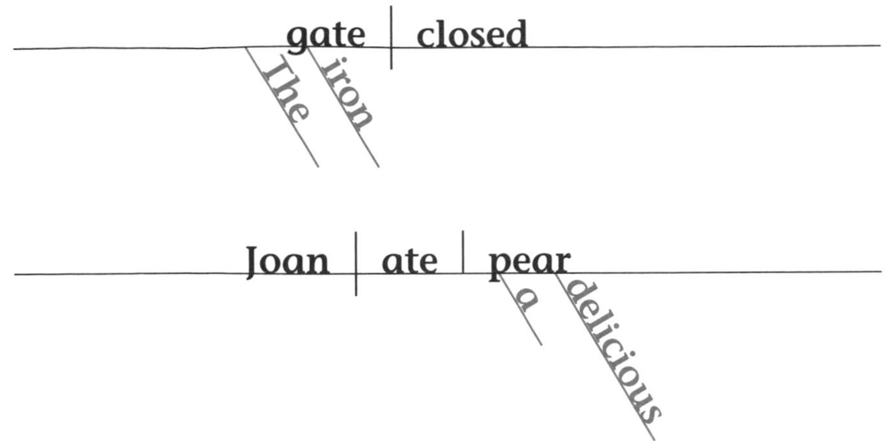

Try It Yourself

Diagram each of these sentences on a sheet of paper.

1. The old clock ticked slowly.
2. The fragile antique glass shattered.
3. The water temperature dropped suddenly.
4. The children built a gigantic sand castle.
5. The pilot landed the jumbo jet safely.

Handbook of Terms

A

abbreviation A short form or a word used in place of the whole word: *in.* for *inch, Sun.* for *Sunday*.

adjective A word that describes a noun or a pronoun.

Adjectives can be used to compare two or more persons, places, or things: *hard, harder, hardest.*

Some adjectives tell exactly how many: *one, two, third.*

Some adjectives tell about how many: *some, few, many.*

The adjectives *a, an,* and *the* point out persons, places, or things. They are called articles.

Common adjectives are all adjectives that are not formed from proper nouns: *red, heavy, shiny.*

Demonstrative adjectives *(this, that, these,* and *those)* point out specific persons, places, or things: *this* man, *that* coat, *these* hills, *those* melons.

Possessive adjectives are used before nouns to show possession *(my, your, his, her, our,* and *their)*: *my* lunch, *her* book, *their* bags.

Proper adjectives are formed from proper nouns. Proper adjectives begin with a capital letter: *Italian* is formed from the proper noun *Italy.*

adverb A word that modifies a verb, an adjective, or another adverb.

An adverb often follows a verb: The boy spoke *calmly.*

Adverbs may indicate time, place, or manner.

- An adverb of time answers the question *when* or *how often: Finally* the rain stopped.

(continued on next page)

- An adverb of place answers the question *where*: Leroy went *outside*.
- An adverb of manner answers the question *how* or *in what manner:* Eisha slept *soundly.*
- Adverbs can compare the actions of two or more persons or things: early, earl*ier,* earl*iest.*

Well is an adverb. *Good* is an adjective.

antonyms Words that have opposite meanings: *quiet, noisy.*

apostrophe A punctuation mark (') used to show ownership: the *cook's* knife, the *girls'* horses.

An apostrophe is used to replace letters left out in a contraction: *wasn't* for *was not, I'm* for *I am.*

articles The adjectives *a, an,* and *the: a* tree, *an* owl, *the* house.

C

capitalization The use of capital letters. Capital letters are used for many purposes, including the following:

- the first word in a sentence: *T*he bell rang.
- names of people: *J*ane *L*ind
- the word *I*
- an abbreviation if the word it stands for begins with a capital letter: *R*ev. for *R*everend
- an initial: *G.* Washington
- the names of the months of the year: *F*ebruary
- the names of the days of the week: *T*uesday
- the first word in the salutation of a letter: *D*ear Bob,
- the first word in the closing of a letter: *Y*ours truly,
- the first word and all important words in titles of books, stories, and poems: A T*ale of* Two Cities, "*B*eauty and the *B*east," "*T*he *S*ecret of the Cat."
- the first word in a quotation: Mother said, "*I*t's time for bed."
- proper nouns and proper adjectives: *A*laska, *A*laskan pipeline

- titles when they come before a person's name: *D*r. *M*artin *L*uther *K*ing, *J*r., *J*udge *B*randt, *M*iss *W*assink

comma A punctuation mark (,) used to make reading clearer. Among its many uses are the following:

- after the salutation of a letter: Dear Megan,
- after the closing of a letter: Sincerely,
- between the day and the year: May 31, 2004
- between the city or town and the state: Dallas, Texas
- to separate words in a series: red, white, and blue
- in direct quotations: "Play ball," he shouted, "and play well."
- after yes and no when they introduce a sentence: Yes, I will.
- to set off words in direct address: Pat, listen to me.

compound word Two words joined to make one word: cutback, hairdo, makeup, ballplayer.

contraction Two words written as one with one or more letters omitted: *doesn't* for *does not, he'll* for *he will.* An apostrophe replaces the letters left out.

D

direct object A noun or pronoun that completes the action of the verb. A direct object answers the question *whom* or *what* after the verb: Teresa bought the *books.*

A compound direct object has two object nouns: The fire burned the *grass* and the *trees.*

direct quotation The exact words of a speaker. The exact words of a speaker are placed within quotation marks: She politely said, *"Thank you."*

E

exclamation point A punctuation mark (!) used after an exclamation or an exclamatory sentence: Wow*!* How lucky you are*!*

H

homophones Words that sound alike but may be spelled differently and have different meanings: *piece* and *peace, knight* and *night.*

I

initial The first letter in the name of a person: *Mary Todd* Lincoln, *M. T.* Lincoln.

N

noun A word that names a person, place, or thing.

A common noun names any person, place, or thing: *baby, mountains, toothbrush.*

A proper noun names a particular person, a particular place, or a particular thing. A proper noun is capitalized: *Eleanor Roosevelt, Lake Michigan, Declaration of Independence.*

A singular noun names one person, place, or thing: *daughter, town, mirror.*

A plural noun names more than one person place or thing: *daughters, towns, mirrors.*

A noun may show possession or ownership: *painter's* brush, *horses'* tails.

A noun may be used as the subject of a sentence: *Mother* is at church.

A noun may be used as the direct object of a sentence: Kim plays *checkers.*

P

period A punctuation mark (.) used in the following ways:

- at the end of a declarative sentence: *Melissa is a lawyer.*
- at the end of an imperative sentence: *Open the gate.*
- after initials: *A. A. Milne*
- after many abbreviations: *in., Mr., Sept.*

possession Ownership.

Singular possession is expressed by adding an apostrophe and *s* to a noun *('s): fox's* lair, *child's* toys.

Plural possession is expressed by writing the plural form of the noun and then adding an apostrophe: *foxes'* lair, *children's* toys.

predicate The part of a sentence that contains a verb. The predicate tells something about the subject: Al *smiled.* Sue *ate lunch at the Japanese restaurant.*

A compound predicate has two verbs: The frog *hopped* and *jumped.*

pronoun A word that takes the place of a noun or nouns.

A personal pronoun names the speaker *(I, me, we, us),* the person spoken to *(you),* or the person or thing spoken about *(he, him, she, her, it, they, them).*

A possessive pronoun shows ownership or possession *(mine, ours, yours, his, hers, its, theirs).*

A singular pronoun names one person, place, or thing *(I, you, he, she, it).*

A plural pronoun names more than one person, place, or thing *(we, you, they).*

Some pronouns may be used as the subjects of sentences: *She* danced at the party.

Some pronouns may be used as the direct objects of sentences: He teaches *me.*

Q

question mark A punctuation mark (?) used after an interrogative sentence: How are you*?*

quotation marks Punctuation marks (" ") used before and after the exact words of a speaker: "Let's go shopping," said Michiko.

S

sentence A group of words expressing a complete thought.

A sentence that makes a statement is a declarative sentence: *Rita has a garden.*

A sentence that asks a question is an interrogative sentence: *Where are you going?*

A sentence that gives a command or makes a request is an imperative sentence: *Follow the leader around the block.*

A sentence that expresses strong feeling or sudden emotion is an exclamatory sentence: *How kind you are!*

A simple sentence has a subject and a predicate.

- The simple subject names the person, place, or thing the sentence is about: The *man* is a fine editor.
- The verb expresses action or being: The child *bought* a toy.

subject The part of a sentence that tells whom or what the sentence is about: *Ed* baked bread. *The climate in the Arctic* is harsh.

A compound subject has two subject nouns: The *dog* and the *cat* are sleeping in the sun.

synonyms Words with the same or almost the same meaning: *buy, purchase.*

U

underline In handwriting, a line marked under the title of a book to indicate italic type: Treasure Island.

V

verb A word that expresses action or being.

The principal parts of a verb are the present, the present participle, the past, and the past participle: *work, working, worked, worked; go, going, went, gone.*

A verb may be regular or irregular.

- The past and the past participle of a regular verb end in *-ed: baked, (has) baked; jumped, (have) jumped.*
- The past and the past participle of an irregular verb do not end in *-ed: sang, (has) sung; wrote, (have) written.*

The present and the past parts of verbs may be used alone in sentences: *He skates. I ran.* The present and past participles must always be used with helping verbs: *He is skating. I have run.* These are the most common helping verbs.

am, is, are, was, were, be, being, been, shall, will, may, can, has, have, had, do, does, did, should, would, might, could, must

An action verb tells what someone or something does.

A helping verb and a main verb make up a verb phrase: *am feeling, is riding, was leaping, has played.*

A being verb shows what someone or something is. It may be a linking verb or a helping verb: They *are* great athletes. They *are* playing well.

A linking verb is a being verb. A linking verb joins the subject to a noun, a pronoun, or an adjective: She *is* the girl. The winner *was* he. They *were* late.

Tense tells when the action of the verb takes place.

- A verb in the simple present tense tells about something that is always true or about an action that happens again and again: She *eats* lunch at noon.
- A verb in the present progressive tense tells about an action that is happening now: She *is eating* lunch.
- A verb in the simple past tense tells about an action that happened in the past: She *ate* lunch yesterday.
- A verb in the past progressive tense tells about an action that was happening at some time in the past: She *was eating* lunch when I saw her.

(continued on next page)

- A verb in the future tense tells about an action that will happen in the future: He *will come* soon.

A verb agrees with its subject. When the subject is a singular noun or a third-person singular pronoun, *-s* must be added to the present tense verb: Zoe *hums.* He *plays* third base.

When the subject is a plural noun or a third-person plural pronoun, the present tense verb does not end in *-s*: The boys *play* ball every day. They *throw* and *catch.*